BOOK VI

DECODING
THE
DOLPHIN'S BREATH

METAPHYSICAL INTERPRETATION

O.M. KELLY

COPYRIGHT

Copyright © 2023 Margret Ann Kelly/O.M. Kelly
Series: Book VI (Revised)
First Published as Book VI in "Decoding the Mind of God",
Margret Ann Kelly/O.M. Kelly, Copyright © 2011.

All rights reserved. This book may not be reproduced, wholly or in part, or transmitted in any form whatsoever without written permission from the author, O.M. Kelly, www.elanea.com.

The author of this book does not dispense medical advice or prescribe the use of any technique as a form of treatment for physical, emotional, or medical problems without the advice of a physician, either directly or indirectly. The intent of the author is only to offer information of a general nature to help you in your quest for emotional and spiritual well-being. In the event you use any of the information in this book for yourself, which is your constitutional right, the author assumes no responsibility for your actions.
Book ISBN: 978-0-6458487-3-1

AUTHOR

Author O. M. Kelly, known as Omni to her clients and students is an accomplished author and international lecturer, on Metaphysics, Philosophy and understanding the Collective Consciousness. Omni consults for Member States of the European Commission as a Conciliation Advisor and Rhetoric Counsellor for other International Companies throughout Europe. Omni now resides on Australia's beautiful Gold Coast, writing books, and works as a Life Mentor and Business Coach.

Omni has dedicated her life to decoding the mysteries of the universe. With a deep knowledge of the biblical agenda, mythologies including ancient Egyptology, Asian principles, and metaphysical insights, Omni has discovered the secret that all stories share a coded hidden metaphysical language. Her seminal work, "Decoding the Mind of God", is a compilation of nine volumes of metaphysical information based on the research into the coded information of the Laws of the Universe, also known as the Collective Consciousness, and represents a groundbreaking contribution to our understanding of the metaphysical universe. Now, all nine volumes are being released as separate, revised books, each offering a unique perspective on the universe's workings. Omni's work has been widely acclaimed for its depth of insight, and her contributions to the field of metaphysics have been groundbreaking.

THIS BOOKLET

"Decoding The Dolphin's Breath" by O.M. Kelly (Omni) is a captivating exploration of the relationship between humans and dolphins. The booklet begins with a poignant account of a real-life encounter between the author and a group of wild dolphins, setting the stage for a deep dive into the spiritual and metaphysical significance of dolphins.

This captivating booklet takes readers on a journey into the heart of the dolphin-human relationship, exploring the ways in which these majestic creatures can help us attune to the power of free will, telepathic communication, and spiritual enlightenment.

Throughout the Laws of Shamanism the wonderful Dolphin in consciousness, represents the attainment we can reach through ourselves earning our freedom of will. This booklet explains the benefits of the dolphins breath—the why and how we use the breath that influences our divine mentality.

Further, it's a story which reveals how the dolphins have taught us the process to be free of fear, and to tap into the Language of Babylon — to understand the language of Earth.

One of the key themes of the booklet is the idea that dolphins are always breathing their total freedom of thought, and the author provides insights into how humans can learn from this remarkable trait. The booklet also invites readers to embark on a journey into telepathic communication with whales and dolphins.

Overall, this booklet offers a unique and fascinating perspective on the metaphysics of dolphins, and will appeal to anyone interested in marine life, spirituality, and the power of the mind.

Includes a written meditation that can help you relax and unwind your mind.

CONTENT

Introduction

Chapter One
The Wonderful Dolphin Species — Page 1

Chapter Two
Free Will — Page 4

Chapter Three
The Dolphin Is Always Breathing Its Total
Freedom Of Thought — Page 8

Chapter Four
Journey Into Telepathic Communication With
Whales And Dolphins — Page 10

Chapter Five
The Metaphysics Of Palsy — Page 13

Chapter Six
Attaining Our Enlightenment — Page 16

Chapter Seven
The Whale — Page 20

Chapter Eight
The Substance Of Prahna Energies — Page 22

Chapter Nine
The Ancient Art Of The Smoking Ceremony — Page 25

Chapter Ten
The Dolphin's Breath — Page 28

Chapter Eleven
The Sound Of The Dolphin — Page 32

Chapter Twelve
Why Dolphins And Whales Beach Themselves — Page 34

Chapter Thirteen
A Meditation   Page 36

Bonus: Excerpt from the book:
"Decoding The Shaman Within", Chapter 1.
My Maternal Grandmother Was An Alchemist,
O.M. Kelly.   Page 43

Bonus: Excerpt from the book:
"Decoding The Laws Of The Universe", Chapter
One. Our Individual Universal Law And The
Laws Of The Universe, O.M. Kelly.   Page 58

Bonus: Excerpt from the book:
"Decoding Sacred Fung Shwa", Chapter One.
The Meaning Of Sacred Fung Shwa, O.M. Kelly.   Page 71

Bonus: Excerpt from the book:
"Power Thought For The Day Oracle Book",
Introduction, How to Use The Book,
15. DOLPHIN—Free Will,
16. WHALE—Conversation and Communication,
O.M. Kelly.   Page 75

Other Books By O.M. Kelly   Page 81

INTRODUCTION

In the vast ocean, an ancient group has captured the imagination and wonder of humans for generations - dolphins. Revered by many cultures and associated with Shamanic law, dolphins embody the concept of "Free Will" within the framework of the Collective Inheritance. This booklet serves as a personal account of my experiences and insights gained through a journey of exploration and connection with these remarkable creatures.

I recount their entrance into my life and how they instructed me in locating my unique resonance – a sonic testament of my individual DNA interwoven with the thoughts of my predecessors, the architects of my existence. The dolphins bestowed upon me the wisdom to transcend my fear, and deciphering Babylon's linguistic patterns to comprehend the language of the Earth.

I embarked on a journey to channel Prahna energy, "Pha-Rha-Nagh," seamlessly through my being and into my telepathic inheritance, harnessing the enduring breath as the conduit for this transformation. Illuminating the mind's innate capacity to grasp this phenomenon, the dolphins guided me through the intricacies of Alchemy, as it intersects and converges into the geometric tapestry of the Universe. Our minds become a ceaseless performance of never-ending energy.

I have included a meditation that can help you relax and unwind your mind.
Omni

CHAPTER ONE

The Wonderful Dolphin Species

Throughout the laws of Shamanism, the wonderful dolphin species of the consciousness represents the attainment we can reach through us earning our freedom of will. The ocean represents the consciousness, and the dolphin is a representation of you releasing your thinking out into that consciousness. Dolphins are the willing mind of the ocean. I liken them to the raft that I hang on to as I ride the stormy seas, whirling my way through to collect my energy. In the beginning of my Metaphysical/Shaman education, I symbolically attracted five white dolphins to me; and, when I was in doubt, they carried me to my next positive world of thought. Two years later, these five white dolphins came into my life on the beach, and they explained other sections of the Collective Consciousness to me for a period of another two years.

When we look at the evolution of the whale, dolphin, and many fish species, we come to realize the importance of their evolution, as they can change their value of group energy to become androgynous, which allows a firmament of completion throughout the whole of their Collective Inheritance.

In order for a newborn dolphin to learn to swim just after birth, it is born with a total belief in and awareness of itself. It takes up to thirty minutes from birth for it to realize its own independence. That dolphin lives totally in its Collective Inheritance (Consciousness), in which it is capable of mirroring the conformity of the world it lives in, and that is its unconscious/higher mind. Buoyancy can only materialize when the mind is focused on itself, and when and where it feels safe in that realm of thought.

Once, when I was undertaking a serious part of my quest, I went for a swim. The weather had been stifling, and the heat was pulling everyone down, so off to the creek we went one hot day; we filled our picnic baskets, took our towels, and thought we would make a day of it. Into the water everyone went, and, very soon, they all seemed to cool off. Laughter started to break out as our thinking changed, and then it was my turn to plunge in. As I waded out into the deeper water and started to swim, I felt as though a bubble was surrounding me, and I felt uneven and out of balance. It became a hindrance, as I found that I could not do the common crawl or breaststroke. Even when I changed my footwork, my kick still pulled me every which way, and I felt I was getting nowhere. I was just like a cork bobbing around in the water, and I seemed to be turning anticlockwise in circles. Needless to say, rather than make an even bigger fool of myself, I decided to get out of the water, and what an effort that became! I really had to push myself out and onto the land, and my body became so heavy that I stumbled out and collapsed onto my towel. It took me a number of minutes to try to regain my composure. I tried again a couple of hours later, and the same thing happened; I just had to realize that my swimming days had come to an end through my genetics reaching a climax of expediency. Through my intellect achieving its own antenna, I have found that I cannot drown. And I had been a swimmer, representing my home state and working as a swimming instructor throughout my teenage years.

I had stepped out of my conscious and subconscious mind and up into the unconscious/higher recognition of the Universal awareness to live a life of perpetual ascension. And this is where I have earned this golden opportunity to receive the answers that most of you are searching for.

The mother of the baby dolphin is there as a support system and source of nurturing. This continues until the baby dolphin can allow its feelings – or security – to link with the movement, sound, pulse, and tone of the ocean; and to acknowledge the ocean to work with its thinking, which allows it to become at one with the ocean and all the oceanic species. This occurs through the hologram that is automatically created through the dolphin's mind becoming harmonized and mirroring back to itself. It releases a tone of mathematics – or codes – that enables it to create a life of perpetual ascension. Its continual state of mind becomes a focused movement which then carries it forward. That is why the dolphin's mouth is open all the way through to its crown. The same explanation relates to the whale and other similar species as well.

***

A quick Metaphysical explanation of the structure of the brain/mind: Our brain has two sides, left and right. Left brain is our logic (conscious mind). The left brain is our masculine side; our ego, our primal fear, and as stated our logic. It represents how we are representing ourselves to others through releasing from within. Our left brain, our conscious self, is responsible for the first and second-dimensional mind. The right brain is our emotions (subconscious mind). The right brain is our feminine side, our inner creativity. We give out to others with the right side, and our energy in motion – or emotion – creates itself from how we are giving and receiving to and from the self. The right brain represents what we are doing to ourselves within, and what we are capable of receiving through ourselves – through our being aware of that giving. Our right brain, our subconscious self; it is responsible for the third dimension and the relationship to the introduction of the fourth dimension.

The balance of both brains is the doorway up into our unconscious/higher mind. The unconscious/higher mind (Soul/Higher Self) is the freedom with which we can tune into ourselves, but only when the other two have balanced through our attitude to our self. We touch and connect to our unconscious/higher mind, as the other two brains encompass the Soul through looking into one another.

CHAPTER TWO

Free Will

Genesis 1:21 states, "And God created great whales and every living creature that moveth, which the waters brought forth abundantly after their kind, and every winged fowl after his kind, and God saw that it was good."

We now understand that the dolphin and whale are among the earliest species to develop through the evolution of the Divine inheritance. We have also come to a unique understanding that the whale, dolphin, bat, bird, and insect all are connected through the sonar that they produce. They all have evolved completely, up into the highest form of the Collective Intelligence, which is the ultimate ascension for us to learn to create in order to release our own intuition up into the unconscious/higher mind. In other words, they all rely on their own manifestation of sonic sound. Sonic sound: When we raise the level of our thinking and therefore vibration, this is when we harmonise our thoughts with the potential of "the all" the unseen where the level of our thought creates and manifests into physical reality, matching the experience.

The story goes that God created the dolphin and whale on the fifth day of our evolution, and the number five (5) through Metaphysical Sacred Numerology, represents the emotion of "freedom". Can you now begin to understand how the freedom of our own Divine will collects itself? This is all through the mathematics collecting through the Sacred Alphabet, and through this equation, the Sacred Numerology steps in to exalt the measurement. Let us digress here and take a look at the world of ballet for a moment. The dance creates an illusion, and, as we watch that dance in motion, we notice that ballets usually have an equal number of dancers of equal numbers on either side of the stage. As they dance, we are watching a field of quantum physics at work. While we focus on the principal dancers, we are automatically drawn into our unconscious/higher mind through our peripheral vision, which is focused on the dancers on either side of the stage. This scene automatically releases our conscious mind up and into our unconscious/higher mind, and we feel our energy changing into a compatible resonance. This harmonizes and balances throughout our conscious, subconscious, and unconscious/higher mind, which then becomes an enhancement to our Collective Mind. So it is with the dolphin, and this is how they live permanently in the unconscious/higher mind.

When a dolphin swims beside a fast-moving ship, the dolphin uses the power – or the energy – of that ship to add to its own energy in order to propel its motivational expertise through the water. That also explains to us the understanding of free will. The thrust, which comes through the belief of its own sexual empowerment, can keep the dolphin's speed equal to the speed of the ship, where the dolphin then has the opportunity to power beyond the ship, through surging into its own free domain – if it so chooses. It is as if an astral restaurant is supplying the dolphin with nourishment from that energy. Free will is the teenager, and it is also the warrior earning his wisdom through achieving his own self-will.

May I tell you a short story of when I was deeply involved in learning to live in my unconscious/higher mind? I was in total absorption of my unconscious/higher energy, and I had to stay that way in order to be able to understand the mathematical resonance that I needed to apply to my thinking for the lessons that I was given at that time – this is how we are trained into understanding the Shamanic principles (i.e., Universal Laws of the Collective Consciousness). At that time, I was studying the Metaphysical interpretations of the Bible, and I was learning to understand the Book of Psalms. Verses 1, 2, and 3 in chapter 1 gave me confidence that what I was doing was right and correct: "Blessed is the man that walketh not in the council of the ungodly, nor standeth in the way of sinners, nor sitteth in the seat of the scornful. But his delight is in the law of the Lord; (which is life's balance) and in his law doth he meditate day and night. And he shall be like a tree planted by the rivers of the water, that bringeth forth his fruit in his season; his leaf also shall not wither; and whatsoever he doeth shall prosper." Once I understood these verses metaphysically, I realized that I was this tree of knowledge, and the Divine gifts that the Lord passed through to me in my silence would always support and strengthen me. (Remember that, through the Metaphysical vibration, the leaves represent the pages in my DNA. They are my history.)

So this meditative mind became my superior knowing, and this is where I had to stay put. My car needed a tune-up, and my son offered to give it a thorough overhaul as my Christmas gift. I did not say no, and, as he went to work on the car, he could not start it, try as he might. He called me outside and asked me how long it had been like that. I got behind the wheel, looked through my inner vision into the motor, turned the key, and, of course, it started. He took over again as I watched him unplug the leads and remove the air filter, and then I wandered off to pull a few weeds out of my garden. The next thing I heard was, "Mum, who put in these points? When did you get this done – was it yesterday?" "No, I have not had the car touched for the last twelve months," I said. "Rubbish, Mum, the car would never have started. These points are brand-new; they've never been opened and regauged. It would have been impossible for you to start it!" "Well, it did play up a bit twelve months ago, but I have been so absorbed in my studies, that I just became my car, and it has started every time I hopped in?" He replied, "What was that, Mum? What are you talking about – is this more of your mystical stuff?" "Never mind, they're open now, and all will be well. Would you like a cup of tea?" I said to him.

So, you see, this is what a focused mind can create on your behalf. The hardest part is the first step! Now do you see how the dolphin has learned how to become one with the ship through the species' evolution? Thus have I been trained to live the same existence as the dolphin!

The dolphin's evolution goes back to a time millions of years before the arrival of the first humans. As a by-product of the killer whale, dolphins became the next species of emotional conversation. The whale, in Shamanism, is the evolution of the word "communication". It represents the conversation, pulse, and tone throughout the Collective Consciousness, and it sends and receives sound only through that sonic level.

Dolphins and whales are an interdimensional species of the same thought. They created their own groups of consciousness, in regard to time; they have evolved through a separate tone or language for each species, yet they are of same mind. There are eighty-plus species of these cetaceous mammals in the ocean, and, through their continual movement, they are anchored into their genetic inheritance and still have the ability to breastfeed their young.

CHAPTER THREE

The Dolphin Is Always Breathing Its Total Freedom of Thought

The year 1976 was a powerful one through the codes of evolution; if you can remember back to that time, an underwater cave was discovered deep in the ocean floor. Through research, marine biologists determined that this cave was where dolphins and whales went to die. In that cave, these scientists found the skeletal remains of dolphins and whales – amazingly, these remains included hooves that were the same as those of cattle! The scientists could not determine the age of these remains.

Did the cow evolve from, or into, the cetaceous mammillae (dolphin or whale)? No doubt, many a night's conversation has pursued this subject. The brain of the whale is of the same measurement as that of the cow. The cow, in Shamanism represents "contentment", so did one of the cetaceous species achieve contentment on the land? My belief is: as it is in the ocean, so it is reverberated onto the land.

I also know that the horn of the cow is registered into the Collective Consciousness through sonic sound. Through us removing their horns, we have taken cows away from their ability to tune in to their own inner strength. This is especially true for the bull: Without his horns the bull loses the power of achieving his own ego, which is his own eclecticism; therefore, he can no longer lead his tribe, and he just spends his life mating with his tribe through our interference – we have robbed the bull of his emotional fortress. Without their own antennae, these animals have become our servants.

That same story relates to the elephant; when we remove their tusks, we automatically interfere with the genetic intelligence of the next evolution of their species. Their consciousness will automatically deplete as their futuristic time evolves. Do you understand how these species have evolved up into the unconscious/higher mind? We are aware that the dolphin has evolved into having the ability to use both brains at the same time through its only having one nostril. Its mouth opens up into the crown area of the head, so the dolphin is always breathing its total freedom of thought. Its brain is permanently in unison, which has come through the balancing of the middle ear, and this is the beginning of the species' creation into evolving up into their sonic sound. The Tibetan masters also teach us how to achieve this "one brain" facility through the teachings of Esoteric Buddhism, where we tune both nostrils into becoming one.

Dolphins take short catnaps just below the surface of the water, and then they slowly rise up in order to breathe. Their breathing is voluntary, so, when they sleep, they only close one eye, which diverts the energy and frees that side of the brain, while the other hemisphere of the brain takes full responsibility. I know a few humans who have this ability as well, especially when watching TV!

We humans have two nostrils, so the energy of our breath goes into both brains. We breathe in through our nose to activate our brain, and this then reshapes and balances our breath into the middle ear. It then vibrates up through our sound waves into the pituitary gland, which measures each thought and rebalances both brains, as we have already learned. This, in turn, exercises and opens up the pineal gland, which is the upper doorway to the unconscious/higher mind. This is the doorway to Ma'at – or our truth. We breathe in through the mouth to help us relax our fear. By breathing through the mouth, we activate the brain, and this exercises our hypothalamus gland, which is the resting place of our fear and the dragons of our past. Keep your mouth closed when breathing in, and your fear will have the chance to release from its past history and disappear! When we close off one nostril, we open up the passages in only one hemisphere of the brain, which then has a chance to activate while the other brain is in abeyance. That abeyance receives autonomically from the other brain, and this is how we enhance our memory to master the next level of thought. Our breath is very important with regard to our mentality releasing and adjusting to its own inner balance. Can you now understand a little bit more as to the intellectual difficulties that we pass on to our next generation?

CHAPTER FOUR

Journey Into Telepathic Communication With Whales and Dolphins

My journey into telepathic communication with whales and dolphins began in 1979, on the day that I took my children to Sea World on Australia's Gold Coast. I was having some difficulties at that time in coming to terms with my own emotional responsibilities. So, while my children went off to play, I chose to sit on the grass under a tree to think about things and rest.

After a while, I noticed a small creek beside the tree. The creek meandered through the park, and, not far from where I sat, was a beautiful little bridge arched across the creek. I got up and walked over to the bridge, stepping onto it so I could look at the water. As I looked down into the water from the bridge, I began to cry, but I noticed that my tears were coming from my right eye only. As I was watching my tears land on the water, a dolphin surfaced beneath the bridge, turning to look up at me. We looked at each other, right eye to right eye. My tears fell into his eye, and then I felt his smile. Gently, gently, gently, God waits for us to realize our own temperament.

That meeting with the dolphin melted my heart and changed my perspective towards myself; it was the beginning of a new doorway that changed my thinking. The dolphin – that distinction of my Spiritual awakening – opened my eyes to feelings that I had suppressed long ago. That event was just prior to my second contact with Extra-Terrestrial Intelligence.

My next meeting with dolphins came in 1989. By this time, my children had grown and left home, and I was alone and on my journey of self-discovery. At six o'clock each morning, I used to take a meditation group to a place on the face of a cliff near my home; this spot overlooked the Great Barrier Reef.

One morning, after the meditation, I felt that there was

something I had left unfinished; but, having appointments to keep, I had to return home. At 10:15 that same morning, just as a client walked out the door, the phone rang, and my next two clients cancelled. I had become very restless, and I knew that I had to go back to the cliff. Friends arrived unexpectedly to invite me to lunch, but they quickly sensed my restlessness. When I told them about my urge to return to the cliff, they all wanted to come with me.

So, off we all went, arriving at the cliff at exactly 11:11 a.m. I walked to the edge of the cliff, and, as I looked down into the water, I saw a pod of eight dolphins – five were white, and three were grey – I had been waiting for many years for those dolphins to come into my life. I knew that they were a gift of consciousness, although, at that time, I did not know what I was supposed to learn from them. All I knew was that, each morning, I had to be there at ten o'clock – and, each morning, those same dolphins returned. I knew that they were connecting to my meridian lines through my lymphatic system. I could feel the subtle changes throughout my mind, and I found that, as I began to understand their thinking, my auric body began shape-shifting into the body of a dolphin.

One morning, as I watched them swim around me, I heard one of the strangest noises that I had ever heard inside my own head, and my right ear began to pulse. I will never forget the pain as my ear banged, popped, hissed, and screamed. The crown of my head felt as though it was going to split open. I know now that I was opening up the channel of communication, which is the introduction into the unconscious/higher mind that is brought through from the Collective Consciousness when we have reached a certain mathematical level in our awareness. We refer to this as the awakening into the Universal language, where we have the possibilities of understanding every language on the earth. I have named this the "Pre- Babylonian Institute".

That pain continued for three long weeks, and, the moment that I doubted my gift, I developed an abscess in my ear – but, the moment I gained my strength back to believe in my gift again, the abscess disappeared. The pain became so bad that I went to the local hospital for help.

As I walked through the door of the hospital, a woman came towards me. She spoke to me in a foreign language, but I understood every word – I actually heard the language change. She had commented on the heaviness of my pain.

After I had received my treatment and was leaving the hospital, a man held the door open for me; he, too, spoke in another language, and I understood him. He told me to go home to bed and rest. Instead, I drove straight back to the cliff and shouted out to the ocean, asking it to carry my thanks to the dolphins for the gift of understanding that they had given me.

I was a beginner at that time, so I had to believe and trust in what the dolphins were trying to communicate to me. I realized that they were introducing me to how I could free my will so that I would not be so bound up by my own constrictions.

I just have to think to them now, and they receive my emanations, through my becoming as they are. My mythical experiences are embedded in me forever.

CHAPTER FIVE

The Metaphysics Of Palsy

Around that same time, I was asked to see a family of two adults and two children, each of whom suffered with different types of palsy. They came from the outback, living many kilometres away from their nearest neighbour, and were asking for help with understanding their dis-ease. Through one of them searching within and questioning themselves, they had been brought to my door. I noticed that each member of the family breathed only through the mouth; the nose was completely closed off in all four of them.

The Metaphysics of palsy is that, as it releases up through the DNA, it creates the strength of feeling ostracized – or of ostracizing from the nation within. This is where we selectively group our thoughts into their tribes and then send them on their way. We do not want the responsibility of rearing any of our personalities (aspects of self), so we pass them off as an offence to self. This is why the dis-ease has been named Bell's palsy.

Once I understood the cellular inheritance of the dis-ease, I knew how to communicate back to the family in a language that, hopefully, they could understand. They were fixed in their thinking, so I had to teach them to look out through another window of the mind in order to be brought back into their own value of self. Through doing that, changes could then begin to occur autonomically.

I found them a house to rent on the outskirts of town, where they could adjust to the sounds of others who lived close by, as, simultaneously, they learned to share their feelings openly with one another.

My telepathic education with the dolphins was becoming clearer as my doubts became less, and I gained the ability to understand their frequencies and hear their language. They seemed to know more about me than I knew about myself! I needed to understand more regarding Bell's palsy, so I asked the dolphins to explain it to me through their Metaphysical interpretation.

Let me now explain a story to you about how we, as humans, can release the free will of self. I will tell this to you in the same way as the dolphins explained it to me, but I will use that family as my example.

There were five houses on the top of a cliff overlooking the ocean, and one house stood apart from the rest – this was the house where I had placed the family – the other four houses had wonderful gardens, each filled with flowers and laughter. The house that stood apart from the others had none of those things, as the occupants were too busy looking through one window, feasting their eyes on the ocean. Over time, their minds became devoid of emotions, and their stares became vacant; no movement stirred in their minds.

One day, a neighbour brought over a basket of vegetables for them, ringing the doorbell and leaving the basket on the front doorstep. The people inside the house that stood apart from the others cautiously opened the door and hesitantly brought the basket inside, eagerly accepting the gift that they had just been given.

Seven days later, another neighbour brought over a basket of vegetables, but this time there was a small packet of seeds at the bottom of it. Those inside were being introduced to another window of their minds, and so they began to look out a window in their house that overlooked the other houses. In other words, they began to tune in their attention to another thought. They thought about that gift of seeds for a while, and then went out to prepare a small garden. When the other neighbours saw the family preparing and watering their new garden, these neighbours, too, brought over seeds – and so the new garden grew. In time, that garden began to reach out and away from that house, growing towards the other houses. The family had an outside interest now, and, as time progressed, their interest in the garden grew; they were beginning to release their freedom, which had been locked up for so long.

Gently, as their responsibility to self began to take second place through their own values, they began yearning for contact with others. They became impatient to return the gifts that they had been given, and so, when the time came, they took a basket filled with their own vegetables over to the neighbours.

When we cannot reach out, we choke off what is within – palsy is a disease that begins with loneliness. Over time, that precious family accepted their plight, and they continued on with smiles on their faces to urge themselves forward. They learned to understand the positive behaviour that they needed in order to express their newly found freedom of releasing and accepting their own will.

CHAPTER SIX

Attaining Our Enlightenment

Before we began this journey of attaining our enlightenment, we needed to search ourselves to realise whether we were free to be able to commit the time to explore the self. What was freedom, anyway? Hadn't we always been free? We were free to speak to others. We were free to accomplish whatever we wanted, so how come things were entangled so much now? Where did we go wrong?

At that time, our lives were dependent on only one or the other hemisphere of our brain. No one had ever explained to us the importance of our thinking. At school, we were taught the stories from everyone else's experience, and we had to base ourselves on how others achieved – it took time for us to mature enough to realize that we could offer something to ourselves. No one explained to me that the two sides of our brain had to work in unison to get us to where we ideally sought to be. No one had ever explained that we had a hidden contract that we carried within us all our lives – and that this contract was for us to use in order to reverse our psyche. It wasn't freedom on the outside that mattered; all that mattered was the freedom to feel and understand ourselves – without worrying what others would think. We had heard about the logic sense that we had to find – and also about the emotional strength that we sometimes felt got in the way. We relied on our competency to create our moments. But we kept on stumbling, and it seemed that the confrontations we had to face had no end; time seemed to stand still, and the mind picked up its own constant inner chatter – as a result, we began turning around in circles, and we could not find any direction that looked to have positive outcome, so we just kept on plodding along.

And then someone would say something to jolt our memory, and this thought kept us alive. It was like a shot in the dark. Time and time again, it would surface, reminding us that we could have a reversal – this could be a turning point in our life. Instead of an anticlockwise movement, we did have the opportunity to move in a clockwise direction. We wanted out of the mess that had slowly been creating itself through our always referring to examples from our past.

We just had to dig deeper; we had to have something to believe in – something to carry us forward and support us – and the only way we knew how to accomplish this was to walk forward. Slowly, over time, we began to note the changes in our thinking; we began to surprise ourselves, and this we know as faith. We came to realize that this quest is here for us to learn how to understand and create our own fulfilment, all by ourselves. Slowly, we began to realize our truth. It is only in the school of "educated thought" that we realize that we have another side to our brain, and it has been sitting in abeyance waiting for us to stop our chatter all along. The higher we reached up inside, the easier it seemed to become to reach even higher; this excited us and gave us the confidence to aim for the highest part of us. There was a huge light at the end of the tunnel, and we found that we were welcome there. No one explained to us that we were reaching for the next evolutionary step of our existence, where our intelligence seemed to drop from the sky. We were manifesting our own sonar, and we could begin to vibrate into our sonic sound; in other words, we were evolving into the dolphin language. We all have this Universal language – it is the design of the human brain – this is what has fortified us into becoming the ultimate of all species on the planet. We need to understand that the energy – or life force – of all of God's creatures has been absorbed by us humans in order to keep us standing upright.

During this time, through my Shamanic education, I noted that, as the dolphins released a thought through their sonic sound, that thought was then transferred through the language of mathematics into English so that I could understand it. At first, the words came through one at a time; this was a slow process that collected over time. (Please remember that I was in shock mode to think that this all could be happening to me. Where the hell was I? La-La Land?). All I can do is to write and explain these gifts of Universal consciousness to you, which, hopefully, will take away your fear when it becomes your turn to tune in to more awareness regarding your own sonic vibration. We all have it! The only reason that you will falter is through the lack of trust in yourself, not through your lack of trust in the Universe. Don't worry what others think! Remember, this experience is not happening to them – they have not yet been selected – and so, while they are noticing your attitude, they still have yet to realize that they need to unblock their own fear. But that is exactly what they must do before they can walk, or work, on the same intellectual level with you.

Those five white dolphins took me into the holographic world of many different types of energies, which were then transformed into geometrical mathematics. Everything was being shown to me in degrees. The ocean species vibrate to 40 degrees through the Collective; each species of evolution has its own set of mathematics to abide by, and it is only when their species' antenna has peaked mathematically, that the next species has the opportunity to evolve.

From there, I moved deeper into sonic sound, where my thinking elevated beyond the ordinary human level. Those dolphins were there to help me to birth up and into my unconscious/higher energy. Remember that everything is placed before you at exactly the right time. This is the creator at work. If you have asked for something – or questioned yourself – and it has not presented itself to you, you are not yet ready to receive. There is more homework for you to accomplish.

Dolphins' movement in the water is permanently arcing through the natural flow of their body movement, and this creates the perpendicular motion that allows them to become their own mathematical creation. As they evolved, their sexual juices had to course through their body to allow the Alchemy to release through their being stimulated into their unconscious/higher energy – and, through all of this, they have attained their buoyancy, which has elevated their perpetuity up into the unconscious/higher mind. Again, I mention Einstein's "Theories of Relativity", where he explains time and space, as to how the arch of the body is creating the gravitational fields in which we move and live. Dolphins have earned their unconscious/higher recognition to be free! We, on the other hand, are still meandering along! We only have to look at the changes over time that our Olympic swimmers have accomplished through changing their movement by introducing the dolphin kick to the breaststroke and butterfly.

That perpendicular motion is always available to dolphins – it has become their life force, and there is nothing that they cannot achieve or produce through their own free will. Maybe here I can add what I have written in another book regarding the mosaics that Schwalla De Lubitz found on the floors of the temples in Egypt. As he was collecting the codes, he found a hidden one of a Pharaoh whose penis protruded from his navel area, which explains exactly what I am writing to you now. In the next evolution of humanity's achievement – that is, for us to accomplish the intelligence of our unconscious/higher mind – we use our sexual energy to attain another advanced degree of intelligence. Read the myths, learn the ancient art of yoga, study the Tibetan breath, and, now for the wisdom of the big one, repeat your times tables that you learned at school (which also opens up your mathematics, and is what education is all about), which will endorse everything I have said to you. Through my dolphin contact, I learned that I have the total freedom of self for every thought that I think.

Dolphins have no legs or hips, so they are free of the strained relationship to the sciatic ("Sky-Attic") nerve. Their tail begins at the end of their spine, just like ours does (if you take note of the beginning of the human evolution, we also had an elongated spine to begin with). Dolphins have an extremely long spine, and their sexuality is in relationship to an apex of one-third to two-thirds. Their perpetual motion creates a sexual rocking movement which enhances the spermaceti organ, to the point where they are living in a permanent state of Spiritual enlightenment.

In other words, they are living the eclectic consciousness: The perfect music that creates the sound of "OM". Dolphins are not bound up with trying to understand who they are. The moment when we achieve that orgasmic print of consciousness is the moment when the orgasm comes home to God, which then ignites the pineal gland – all of which produces the somatic enhancement of the mind.

CHAPTER SEVEN

The Whale

Years ago, man hunted the whale for its blubber, which man used for many things. Man rendered the blubber down into oil, and, in the process, discovered the white oil gland of the whale. Originally, it was thought that this gland was filled with sperm; hence, the name "spermaceti' ("sperm whale"). That fluid is the ectoplasm that has built up through the whale's commitment to its own Oracle; it has been created through the movement of its eternalness through its own energy.

If you care to look into the pineal gland and the function of its own understanding, you will realize how the whale's Spiritual awareness becomes the "essence" that pronounces its own intellectual energy back to itself. This is exactly the same story as to how we accomplish our own enlightenment! When I walk down the street – and walk through many people – my inner vision alerts me to the levels of intellect of those people. This is symbolically delivered through the forehead. In other words, you are delivering, to those who know, your myth of what you have accomplished throughout your life.

Whales have shown us their migratory path, which they have travelled continuously for thousands of years. Those "song lines", as the Aborigines call them – or "paths of light" – can be seen from satellites that move well above the earth. These "lines" have collected on the ocean floor, and the whales tune in their frequencies of sonic sound to these "lines" for migration purposes. These whale "lines" are pathways that also hold the sonar of the earth's magnetic grids together. These are energy ley lines that must not be interfered with.

The sperm whale can dive to a depth in excess of 3,000 metres, and it can stay underwater for 120–160 minutes. Through the Sacred Numerology, that equation is 3 x 40 to 4 x 40 (remember that the ocean vibrates at 40 degrees), depending on the whale's condensed consciousness. That is another code of recognition. Do you see the strength of the unconscious/higher mind and its capabilities? The oceanic consciousness vibrates through the hierarchy to the number forty (40). The movement of the ocean is at 40 degrees, and the fish and oceanic mammals connect to themselves through this same 40 degrees. The floor of the ocean corrects and balances itself through the number forty (40) – whether this is 40 degrees, 40 minutes, 40 hours, 40 days, or 40 years – the ocean can never change the mathematical value of its vibration.

Once the code has been recognized and accepted throughout the whole of the Collective Consciousness, the rest of the codes can evolve and move up from their previous degrees. That is evolution!

CHAPTER EIGHT

The Substance Of Prahna Energies

My next step was to learn how to bring the substance of Prahna ("Pha-Rha-Nagh") energy through my body and into my telepathic inheritance, as well as how we are able to achieve this through the eternal breath. The dolphins showed me how the brain is able to realize this phenomenon through the Alchemy squaring and arching into the geometric hologram of the Universe. This allows us to keep our mind in a repetitive performance of never-ending energy.

Prahna energy is available to us all as we coincide with and through the Collective. It is the spherical sparks of light – or minute holograms – that we are able to induce from the atmosphere of the planet. This energy feeds our alchemical responses, which are then compounded into our aura. Prahna energy supplies our intelligence with an elevation into the worlds beyond. As the crown of our head aligns and opens up into the crown of the Universe, we are permanently in an etheric domain of intelligence. The mind of the dolphins helps them accomplish their great speeds through the ocean by aligning their energy with their thoughts.

Those dolphins also taught me how to find and chant my own tone, which is heard right around the planet. Through a state of endearment to self, I wanted to hear my own sound, so I had to find the sound that came from deep down inside my body, where the three Metaphysical Gods of the ancient myths – "EL," "AN", "EA" – could communicate with one another in the same resonance. We refer to our whole self as the "Mind, Body, and Soul" – or the "Father, Son, and Holy Spirit", which is collectively called the "Mind of God".

Once I found my sound, I could then follow its harmony, bringing it up into my mouth, nose, and eyes, which allowed it to create its own path through the sonic system, and up to the crown in order to open up into the supra consciousness and beyond. This was a testing time for my patience, as I thought I was more than ready for this next shift; once again,

I expected it to work instantly.

Again the burning sensation of pain came through me – and, please, remember that a strong pain is an erratic conversion of steroids that have collected and have nowhere to go. This time, it was mostly around the sinus area and up through the nose, which was in order to align my olfactory system with my new intelligence as it began to correlate with my thoughts. I had to trust much deeper in order to allow the changes to be made within my cellular structure. When my cells were ready to relate to their new consequences, so, too, was my truth ready to release to me. In other words, my inner and outer worlds had to become one; both hemispheres of my brain had to view one another within their continual séance.

When I finally heard my true voice chanting, it sent shock waves of loving feelings into every cell in my body. I never wanted it to cease. I realized that the whole of creation was accepting me! They had heard my voice! I was teaching myself through the belief and trust in self that I had earned. We refer to that chant as the "Aum" – or "OM" – of the intelligent Universe. In Arabic, it is pronounced as the "Oum of Allah". The muezzin – or, pronounced correctly, the "Mo-Adz-An" – is the man who calls Muslims to prayer five times per day to anoint themselves. On a recent trip to Turkey, I journeyed with sixty of my European students so that we could travel the ancient pathways of the Silk Road. One day, while I was conducting a seminar, the midday prayer was pronounced. My students and I had the pleasure of listening to 150 simultaneous calls coming from the mosques surrounding us. The sound came into the room and echoed around the walls in a pristine condition. I stopped talking, and we all were amazed at the clarity of the Divine sound surrounding each one of us.

When the prayer finished, I opened my eyes to see everyone with tears in their eyes through the beauty they had felt in that moment. Through the silence we felt within, we each received the sound according to where our mind had attained its higher level. If this was an introduction into the heavenly realms, none of us should have any fear left in our bodies. The ego could feel complete. The vibrations that we were feeling allowed us to receive these higher energies of what we refer to as the "Essene Masters". Through the subtle sounds, the glands in the neck area were harmonizing with one another, and we were swept up into the echo of the light of the Collective – into the unconscious/higher mind.

***

Explanation in relation to the three Metaphysical ancient Gods: "EL", "AN", "EA". Interpreted through the matter of physics—or the Metaphysical language – these three names are here to remind us that we can attain Everlasting Life, Ascending and Nourishing, with an Energetic Attitude. All this is similar to how we introduced our self into our spoken word, which was released to us through our DNA. The first dimension of the Metaphysical God "EL" (Everlasting Life), which represents the home of our ego in relationship to our sexual encounters. These encounters are our basic structure of searching for a placement of our own responsibilities. This is the first doorway to where we connect to our lungs of consciousness, which is where we understand the breath of our inner worlds. Our next evolution is into the Metaphysical God "AN" (Accepting and Nourishing), where we have understood our primordial earlier worlds through collecting our intelligence and accepting the possibilities of harvesting the seeds we have already sown (our thoughts and deeds). You have entered up into your education system, which is your inner university. Automatically, this subconscious awakening brings the information up and through to your heart, which opens you up into a belief that you can accomplish anything your mind desires. The combination of this energy then traverses up to connect us into the highest form of intelligence – our unconsciousness/higher mind – that is, to the Divinity of the Metaphysical God "EA", which, through the earlier language, was pronounced "He-ia" (Heavenly Energy of Intelligence Ascending). This is the last of the three Metaphysical prime Gods that we connect to, and it is the home of our heavenly kingdom, which is situated around the crown of the head. It is where we realize that the Laws of the Universe have a purpose for each and every one of us, and that we all have the ability to reconnect back into the origin of our Soul.

CHAPTER NINE

The Ancient Art Of The Smoking Ceremony

Another causal point that we should understand in its correct behaviour is the ancient art of the smoking ceremony that one gives to oneself, and I realized the power of it on my last trip to Egypt. My hotel room looked out over a quadrangle that had designated areas called the "Oum Palace" ("Place"), where men could pause from their work to take their individual resonances and smoke their pipes. That quadrangle was hosed in the morning before and after the ceremony, and then again in the afternoon, and yet again in the evening.

That special time is when men like to atone to themselves, with their Almighty, and take their respite up and into their higher mind. It frees the stress that can become entangled throughout the body. It is the renouncement of self. It is a baptismal rite that we give to our own Alchemy in order to equate the mind.

When they finish smoking, they thank themselves for the gift that they have received. There are very few cases of cancer registered with these people, as they are permanently anointing themselves through the ritual of receiving from God.

We are trying to erase this atonement from the planet by restricting the flow of the inner self, and we do so through what we still do not want to understand about ourselves. Essence from the smoke through inhalation multifacets the Alchemy that we produce, which is then brought up into the brain through the two energy holes that are in the upper roof of the mouth.

This also relates to everything we eat and drink! It is where the essence of our food releases when we chew, and this filters through into the brain. The chemicals that we manifest are equated for the use of cellular regeneration. That essence is here to work with and through us. The smoke from the cigarette or pipe comes from the essence of the tobacco plant, which is all related to the tomato plant. The tomato is called the "love apple", so, really, no more explanations are needed.

It is amazing how many times I have been advised to give the codes of tobacco, through my radionics machine, to non-smokers who come to me for healing! I write the code of the number onto those clients' pieces of plastic, and they are happy with the mathematics. Those people are usually extremely stressed; they work most of their lives for others, giving themselves no time to nurture the self. They rely on glancing at the Oracle of their mind, where they are looking at their own reflection with blinders on.

Why does a person take up smoking? To satisfy the research station of our ego, we reach up for the ultimate essence to help us accumulate our own self-worth. It releases in us a sense of resurrecting our choked-up thoughts. We are known to place ourselves too far ahead of our thinking, where we expect an immediate answer. If the answer is not given, the next thought is piled on top, and, if that one is not answered, then away we go again. The mind becomes jammed, and so the lungs do, too, because the energy cannot harmonize and balance itself. Our lungs represent the flow of our breath. Hence, the mythical interpretation of the dragon, with smoke coming out of his nostrils.

I remember my soft-spoken Uncle Dan, whom I loved dearly for his gentle and serene wisdom. He was a philosopher. When he was ninety-nine years and nine months of age, I asked him why he smoked. He told me that he had been smoking tobacco since he was fourteen years old, and it had become a great companion to him. He said that, over the years, he and the tobacco had come to appreciate the relationship they had with one another. The next day, after smoking his last pipe, he laid it on a tray, settled down under his blanket, and died. There was no cancer; his lungs were clear. I remember that story because, as a young woman, I had felt guilty for asking him so many questions the day before he died. I know he died happily, because he still had the same gentle smile on his face when we walked into the bedroom and found him.

So let us set this story straight regarding lung cancer. Lung cancer is brought on through the refusal to breathe and acknowledge the thought of the moment! Through their own pressure, those people have a tendency to draw harder on the tobacco, and so the chemicals of that plant are multifaceted into the tissue. Now, if both of those energies were used in unison, there would not be a problem. Learn to say thank you for the gift you have announced to yourself – and remember to do so when you next place your cigarette butt in the ashtray.

Let's remember Sir Winston Churchill and the Queen Mother, two supreme Elders of the English hierarchy, both of whom lived past 100 years of age, and both of whom smoked for most of their lives. They lived for so long through their emotional intellect being announced to self and others with a balanced mind to the theme of the subject that they were discussing; therefore, no stress developed in the mind, and no stress needed to recreate itself in the body! The choice to smoke is yours; so, please, get your thinking right. Ever since we learned to stand upright, we have eternally resurrected our thinking – and we are still doing so, to this day. No one can forbid anything to anyone else, and this is the reason why, when we live in doubt, we reach out to search for support through the eternal species!

CHAPTER TEN

The Dolphin's Breath

The dolphin is a playful and excitable creature, free with a childlike innocence, it finds the rebellion and power of a teenager in order to live and express those urges in the moment.

In my Metaphysical/Shamanic journey with the dolphins I undertook their guidance to explore different concepts and experiences. The experiences of motion that I learned from each lesson took many months for me to achieve, as I had to search within to see where the difficulties of motion were between the dolphin's evolution and our own. What had they gained that we could not? What freedom did we create for ourselves that would become a hindrance to the level that they already had attained through their intellect? I could only begin to understand the evolution of their emotional intellect once I had explored these questions. It was a fun time in my life, with much laughter, and many other humans wanted to share the responsibility of this education with me.

I learned to understand about the pressures around the crown of the head and the coordinates of the templates of the skull, which are pressure plates that work exactly the same as the tectonic plates beneath the ocean floor.

I experienced birthing gills, flippers, a dorsal fin from my spine, and a blowhole at the top of my skull. I watched as my skin changed its proportions, and I could feel the mathematical movement that gave me this waterproof bodysuit, which created the movement of razor-sharp skin that would create my swiftness; I could even feel scales producing themselves all over the surface of my body. Once I understood the value of their emotions, I evolved through the quantified movement of all the species of the ocean very quickly.

I was quite amazed when they showed me how to birth my gills, which are separation chambers we align with, and these are situated just under the shoulder blades. The same capacities that gills have are situated in the top of the lungs of us humans. All this is part of the education into the ultra Shamanic responsibilities, where we understand the codes of co-creation with the unconscious/higher mind. Darwin was right, you know!

Every species on the earth has the same structure of this concise development, which is echoed throughout the human evolution, where we must construe and answer back to equate both ourselves and all the other species; it is then released out of our hands through the Divine mathematical equation and returned into the Collective Consciousness. I now use those same coordinates in cranio-sacral therapy. Through Shamanism, it is the Chinese crane ("Kha-Rha-An") energy, and that wonderful bird has the crown of its head opened to these elements of the Universal Laws. Through the Egyptian principles, it is the same story as the He-Nu – or the Bjn Bjn bird – that is carved in many of the hieroglyphs. Nothing on this planet is unknown to us.

The next step for me was to watch and learn about my breathing. Slowly, I began to understand how my breath was capable of changing through the thoughts of the moment. If my thought was positive and in my truth, it blew to the right side; if I released a negative thought, it blew to the left, and so I began to understand what it was creating through the electromagnetic force fields. These are the fields of our aura releasing an electronic charge, which is like the waves of a radio signal bouncing off mountains. This gave me a clearer understanding of how our pituitary gland has the ability to do justice to our thinking. Also, we could use this information in regard to how these fields of energy manifest the weather patterns.

Then I had to understand which section of the brain was urging me through its cleavage, forcing me to bow to its control, as this is how the dolphins use the energy of the ocean. I was beginning to understand the energy of both brains; I was starting to realize how I could think a thought and watch the transference of which brain was activating first. I now use this energy of the ocean with children who have a learning difficulty, and for the child to become aware of their breathing. I place the responsibility back with the children, so that they can learn to become conscious of their breathing and see within for themselves which hemisphere of their brain is overtaking their thinking. Children are very flexible, and they are quick to size up a situation; it does not take them long to accept the challenge of learning to master their own lives. Their mental difficulty becomes a thing of the past very quickly, once they understand that they are in control of their own behaviour. This process opens up the mathematics, which is situated at the base of the brain.

Dolphins communicate with one another by using the crown of their head. Their crown is permanently opened, and so their telepathic inheritance becomes their light – or intelligence – and it is permanently activated, which again equates to the number forty (40), the value of the oceanic vibration.

Through the dolphin's breath, we learn to open up our mind naturally and permanently. Some of you reject this through your fear, thinking that if we leave our energy open, somebody might come and attack us from within, or take over our bodies. That is all a fallacy. The only attack that occurs is you returning your fear back to you. The shadows of your old thoughts must disappear, which allows you to clear the path for your new confidence to create its own light and abundantly walk through you.

I was beginning to realize and release my Prahnic breath just as the dolphins had taught me to do. I was to draw in my breath through my nose, learn to hold it without any pressure, and then slowly release the breath back out into the consciousness. Through doing that over and over again, my breath became longer, and I found that I was breathing from deep within my stomach.

Through the roll of my inner circle elongating and strengthening itself, my breathing took longer and longer, and I became stronger and stronger. I learned that my concentration was focusing in a perpetual movement, and, the more I trusted in me, the deeper my breath released the pressure in my lower intestines. I could believe in this consciousness of light and trust myself with much more enthusiasm and reliability.

I realized that I was beginning to release my own Oracle; my visions were shape-shifting into geometric symbols, through my energy moving into a consequential relationship to all that is.

The dolphins also showed me their body movements, by way of my swimming through a gelatine bath, which represented the pressure of the ocean. You cannot move forward in a straight line through gelatine, as the pressure is too great. Dolphin movements have to be made in a curve, as they roll their energy from side to side; they rotate through the waves of consciousness using the mathematical cyclic code of 40 degrees. Why? They have evolved with flippers, not arms, and they can rotate with a permanence of motion through the continuance of that sacred number, which vibrates through the ocean.

Dolphins rely on their understanding – which is our legs – and they force their body to connect to their crown. This is also the coded equation of the relationship to all the species of the ocean. It is why a fish must twist as it moves in order to swim, and why it sleeps with its eyes wide open when it is still. The ocean becomes a solidified mass of energy around the species that inhabit it, and yet they can breathe through it all. It is like a state of suspended animation. That is the sway we need in order to keep our energy in a propelling motion. It was a marvellous learning. Now do you understand how the serpent became a symbol of trigonometry?

CHAPTER ELEVEN

The Sound Of The Dolphin

Dolphins are the will of their own life force; they have no fear. The sound of the dolphin vibrates at a range of 2-4 megahertz, which is equivalent to human energy. In the human vibration, the vagina and penis vibrate at 2 megahertz. As the vibration increases, in multiples of 2 (i.e., 2 x 2 = 4 megahertz, and so on) all the way up the spine, it releases the sexual hormones that are created through the pituitary gland, which builds up to release in us a climactic orgasm.

When the vibration of the orgasm builds up in the human form, at that moment, every human on the planet can unconsciously feel those pulses, and equate and balance the energy within themselves. This is a vibration of the Collective Consciousness – an eclectic (a religious experience) invasion of our consciousness, synchronizing through the consciousness of all.

A whale calls at a frequency of 2 megahertz throughout the depths of the ocean, and every other whale in the ocean senses and hears that same vibration as it bounces along the ocean floor. The whale is our connection to the communication of the Collective Consciousness. Their direction and sonic sound come all the way up from their vagina or penis, and that is how that sonic boom can reverberate and be felt completely around the planet.

The same vibration on land comes from the elephant, which also calls at 2 megahertz. That frequency of sound bounces along the ground, and every other elephant on the planet receives the vibration. We have, within our coding, the energies of all the creatures on the earth, and so we become their mirrors. Thus, we must accept and collect to add to the value of the Collective, which also enhances the holographic impulse of every species.

The manta ray is the harmonic balance of the ocean; its energy moves in a complete 40-degree cycle. It travels the oceans, usually alone, once it has reached its maturity. It creates its pods – or students – and it teaches and separates from them again and again. Mantas are the masters of the ocean. Similar to us, as we earn the sacred – or secret – law, they come together and have a meeting, and then they go their separate ways, alone, to teach their students – and the cycle repeats over and over again. They are always in telepathic agreement with one another, working through different sections of their consciousness. When the call goes out, they collect to have another meeting, and afterward, they go out alone again. And so on.

CHAPTER TWELVE

Why Dolphins And Whales Beach Themselves

I would like to explain why dolphins and whales beach themselves. I experienced this throughout my journey: five different times over a period of many years. It happened wherever I was situated at the time, and it did not matter which country I was in. The whales followed the measurements of my unconscious call; they measured my emotional crisis of the moment. When I felt weak, they were there to replace my own shortcomings and supplement me with their strength. I never called them; they just arrived. Each time it happened, I had to count the numbers in the pod that had beached in order to realize the gift that they were returning to me. I learned to look through the codes of those numbers to understand the hidden message.

I then had to supplement my intelligence, depending on whether it was dolphins or whales that had beached, as each related to a different mindset of truth. Before my wisdom had extended itself, I became acutely aware of the tribulations I had to overcome in my next moments. It was a warning for me through the Poseidon energy. The ocean species measure with the Collective Consciousness, and, when we are in doubt, they freely return their energy to supplement that same weakness in ours. They follow the emotional ley lines of Collective Energy, through the awareness of humanity.

Do you recall this happening in your area? What was revealing itself to the consciousness that allowed these creatures to step in to surrender their life for the humans in your locale? Do you recall the 220 dolphins and whales that beached themselves off the Australian coastline four days before the devastating tsunami that struck the shores of Southern Asia? The collective governments of the world had reached a zenith at that time; and, as always, Karma steps in to remind us of our responsibilities. What were they trying to instigate in those nations that was not for the benefit of all concerned? This shows the Universal Laws at work!

Look around and take notice the next time these animals beach in your area – see for yourself. This same reasoning can be related to volcanic eruptions, earthquakes, cyclones, and hurricanes. Please don't think that the force of God/Collective Consciousness is useless; every thought that we think is collected, measured, and very positively returned back to us. We reap what we sow. The higher the responsibility one must stand up for, on behalf of the populace, the greater the Karma returns, in order to return to that land.

CHAPTER THIRTEEN

A Meditation

When we wish to open a doorway of future inheritance, we bring our energy inside our self and close the door to the outside. It becomes a precious thought that you and your Divine Inheritance may collect for the growth of self. This is one of the secrets of asking the Universe for something.

If you want to achieve something, empower it to become yours. If you want to earn something, earn it throughout yourself and learn how to become it; the responsibility is then yours. When you have reached the limits of the intelligence of just one thought, it is given free rein throughout the fields of geometric alignment. You create what you are to becoming your own master.

Here is a meditation to use whenever you would like to ask the Universe to escort you into understanding your freedom in the moment. The meditation opens you up to the eternal consciousness and helps you to release the fear that you have wrapped around yourself for your protection. I rely on my "escort service" to supply me with extra confidence so that I can release these layers, where they can reshape and become an added value to my thoughts.

This meditation should take you about twenty minutes to visualize; but, if you keep practicing, that time will lengthen, until you become it. Have a friend read it for you or record it for yourself:

Settle down on the floor, and give yourself room to move. Close your eyes.

Take three long deep breaths, and empty your mind.

Breathe in. Breathe out.

Breathe in. Breathe out, and feel the length of breath extending.

Breathe in. Breathe extending out to come from deep within your centre, to create a circle of energy that elongates all by itself.

Allow all your worries to be released from your mind, in order for these next few minutes to become yours. Claim your space in the consciousness; there is enough room for you and your thoughts to become one. Allow your mind to visualize that you are standing in front of the ocean. It is a nice sunny day with a soft warm breeze blowing gently on your face.

The ocean is waiting in front of you, so that you may enter into its realms where the waters are calm, warm, and peaceful.

Can you hear the waves lapping at the shore, coercing you to come in and join with another realm that is a parallel enhancement of your own consciousness?

Allow your body to move down into the water, and then float out far beyond the shoreline.

You are now gently wrapped and protected in the arms of the ocean, so feel your body becoming lighter and more buoyant.

Float gently and smell the clean, fresh, salty air.

You are now resting; you are cleansing and relaxing every muscle and cell in your body.

Feel your body sway with the ebb and flow of the tide.

Feel your body rise and fall with the swell of the ocean.

As your body slowly absorbs the senses of the water, allow yourself to slip gently below the surface.

Feel the oxygen around your skin; there seems to be layer of air between you and the water.

Look at the tiny bubbles that are bouncing off your body and gently moving up towards the surface. Have no fear; we are moving into a meditational experience, between you and the dolphins.

Always remember, you are never alone.

Just in front of you, there are five beautiful white dolphins, with bright open smiles, coming towards you.

Watch how they rotate their bodies. Do you sense their movement of ease? Notice how their movements are very fluid. There is no panic, just a gentle roll.

Relax now, and allow all your emotions to sway into becoming that dolphin energy.

Watch as your body begins its transformation into a dolphin, a whale, or any other species that comes into your vision to release itself to you.

Breathe deeply, trust in your visions, and allow the image inside your nation to show you how.

If you have allowed yourself to become fish energy, then feel your gills opening up so that you have the ability to breathe underwater. Those gills are situated on your back just below your shoulder blades.

Take your time; there is no rush – you cannot drown when you have allowed yourself to be placed in the arms of your God within.

You are just remembering an emotion of what you have already attained for yourself to inherit.

Feel your spine relaxing and realigning into a peaceful sentience, and feel the pressure releasing itself from each one of your vertebrae.

Feel each of the vertebrae opening up, one by one, releasing your fears of the expectations that others have over you – or are they the expectations that you have placed on yourself, but have not yet found the strength to uphold?

It will all come together at the right time.

Feel that energy relaxing the tense muscles in your arms and legs.

Sink deeper into the ocean gently now, to where there is a shelf of rock just an arm's length away from you. On that shelf, moving gently with the ebb and flow of the ocean, are a number of wonderful dazzling golden discs waiting for you.

Reach out with your right hand and place them in your left hand, so that we can begin the transformation of you realigning with your DNA.

I would like you to place a disc of gold between each one of your vertebrae, and watch as a shining light comes up through your spine one disc at a time, reaching all the way up to the back of your head.

Feel the difference, as your spine realigns and releases the emotional energy that you have suppressed for such a long time.

Now we will watch how you can begin to swim and learn to breathe in the dolphin's breath.

Roll in and roll out

Roll in and roll out.

Feel your body becoming lighter and more flexible as you swim through the depths of those responsibilities that you have allowed to keep their hold on you.

They are becoming freer to release and move on; there is no longer a stricture of your thoughts confining them to you.

Believe in your own freedom. Feel the release of your lower back and hips through you realizing your old thoughts of restriction; they have supported you for such a long time.

Feel the dolphin's energy as it swims alongside you.

Can you see the golden light from your discs bouncing and reflecting throughout your body?

Now watch that light bounce around the dolphins as you roll in their energy and then roll out of it again.

Allow your mind to wander now.

Over to your right, you will see a pod of three whales swimming gently towards you.

As they move closer, notice the difference in their movement compared with that of the dolphins.

The whales move much more slowly as they roll and release, roll and release, roll and release.

Watch them for a moment.

Can you see what is happening? They, too, wish to communicate with you.

Listen now as the largest whale in the pod speaks to you.

Feel the vibration of its sound as it gently enters every cell in your body.

That whale is asking you to become silent and to still your mind.

Let it converse with you.

Allow its thought to join with yours, as you allow yourself to believe in the language of Cosmic Communication.

That whale is also one of the personalities of your own evolution, reminding you of who you are.

It is a part of the nature of God, it is how he has gathered this energy to sustain and support us, as we prepare each thought for our own endurance.

Allow each cell to be in attendance and every thought to be in abeyance. Your freedom is gently releasing and massaging you, where you have been given a choice to reinvest in yourself.

Let go and indulge in those lights of love, and this will guide you into finding the freedom of your will in order for you to converse much more comfortably with yourself.

That is the gift that they can return to us, when we feel that we have lost our own sense of direction.

Converse with your own personalities – and with others – through confidence in self; communicate with yourself, and trust that, what you have asked for, you also have the ability to receive.

You are in the business of promoting your future right now, and this is all being transformed in your own silent sentience.

Keep your mind steady and still, and allow the awakening of this moment to gather and grow, through the intellectual inheritance that you owe to your self in order for you to be free.

It is waiting for you to touch your inner home, for you to hear through your heart and Soul.

When you feel that you have collected your message from the whale, let that new you measure its self inside you, where you can ascend your life with a newly found confidence.

Now gently close the door of your mind, gather that message, and place it around your heart, where the hands of God will gather it up.

Watch now as the whales swim out of your view, and hear the sound of the dolphins welcoming you back into their realms – their home.

Look at the smiles on their faces; they are so happy with you and how you have found the courage to reinvest in yourself.

Your truth can now become your strength, which holds you upright and becomes a source of light. Your light can become your free will, which will then allow you to live your life free of expectations.

And now I want you to thank the ocean, the whales, and the dolphins, as you exalt yourself up into a new expectation, in order for you to know that this moment has now passed, and you will have the determination to go on.

Watch as your mind allows the next moment to birth itself. Let it show you what you are capable of receiving from yourself. Trust and believe that this investment will continue to grow and support you forevermore.

Those golden discs that you have placed between your vertebrae are there for your keeping.

When you are ready, bring yourself up to the surface of the ocean and gently swim towards the shore. Let your flippers do the work.

Lie down on the shore and rest for a moment. Feel the warmth of the sun as your body returns back to its human form. Allow your memories of this experience to be free to come to you whenever you need to reinvest in yourself.

Open your eyes when you are ready, and wiggle your toes.

Open your mind to these secrets of the Universe and become them, through transforming yourself; they are no longer a secret – they are the recorded message that is embedded in every cell of you, and, more importantly, they are yours to endow.

If the meditation is difficult for you, read these pages again when you are in bed curled up ready to go to sleep. Allow these words to be the final ending of your day, and pleasantly dream on.
Omni

Excerpt from the book:
"Decoding The Shaman Within", Chapter 1.
My Maternal Grandmother Was An Alchemist,
O.M. Kelly.

***
Chapter 1.
My Maternal Grandmother Was An Alchemist

My maternal grandmother was an Alchemist, she was a very powerful and charismatic woman. When she spoke, she held peoples respect and they stopped their inner mind chatter and listened to her. She was a marvelous story teller; her listeners were enthralled with her speech. Her herbal and spiritual knowledge was a part of my daily life. When anyone walked into her house, the overcoats of their persona, (those feelings of fear they had wrapped around themselves) fell off at the front door immediately, all of their layers disintegrated and they were left standing naked in their spiritual garment; which when decoded through the sacred language their inner language, is explaining to them that they are baring their truth, as they know it to be, to others in that moment. In other words, they are not hiding behind their excuses that they use, to support them as they walk forward into their future.

We lived a long way out of the small town that had a mercantile store that supplied us with petrol and farming needs. We killed our own meat and grew our own vegetables and fruit, we preserved and bottled and pickled and salted and made brawn, we relished and made chutney, and created the finest jams and marmalades. You could smell the aroma of our fresh baked cakes and pies for miles. Our puddings were as light as a feather and as sweet as a kiss. We made our own candles and soap to wash ourselves therefore we became quiet self sufficient.

We had our own church service in our large sitting room every Sunday. People travelled for hours to attend our services and when you walked in the sitting room, you could smell the lavender, peppermint, rosemary and rose essences. A roast lamb was slowly cooking in the large combustion oven to be enjoyed as a meal once the service was over.

On a very hot day when you walked into each room, you could smell oranges, lemons, grapefruit; the essences from the odors of the fruit cooled our body down. The oranges were studded with whole cloves, there was something about the two odors blending and harmonizing with one another. The lemons were studded with the bark from the cinnamon tree that one of the elders had brought the seeds back from his journey overseas and the mandarins were studded with a crushed nutmeg.

My mother was not interested in my grandmother's ways. My mother was the needle worker and embroiderer. She made blankets for the beds, the rugs for the floors, and was a marvelous cook. We had the finest tablecloths, always white and starched, with crisp white damask napkins, placed in bright silver rings.

My father was interested in my grandmother's ways. When time permitted he sat for hours and listened, as my grandmother explained her ways to him. As a child, I would walk past the sitting room which seemed dark to keep the heat out and watch their animation. They seemed to be in their own world, where they could only see and hear one another. They spoke softly to one another; they never raised their voices. No one would dare to disturb them. It is a beautiful memory. As I grew up, she turned to me and initiated me into many of her ways. I am so sorry now, that I only half listened some of the time. I listened to her words, but I never heard the words register in my inner alphabet (the words we would use, when we are busily thinking our thoughts). Therefore, the memories were scant, they come back to haunt me now that I have opened up more of my DNA in small glimpses and her words continue down to me from that moment. What I thought I had forgotten was still there embedded in me, just waiting for the opportunity to serve me, when it was needed.

My father was an Elder of our church and also a healer. My uncles were also Elders of the church. Since his Passover, my father has still been a wonderful guide to show me my way; especially in explaining the biblical agenda. He provides insights for me to change my mind to see metaphysical interpretation in other easy. It is just a word here or there, enough to encourage me to create and expand my thinking.

Our Christianity was in every moment of our lives. I heard the Biblical stories explained lovingly through my family, which we all still remember to this day. I left home when I was seventeen; I went out into the world and fell in love and finally married and my life continued.

I remember that my grandmother had over one acre of garden around her house and as a child, I would walk with her as she gathered her flowers and herbs to decorate the table and her cooking was always exquisite to the pallet. For the setting on the breakfast table we would have a vase of freshly cut herbs, which would release their essence to strengthen our thoughts for the day. These herbs were used in the forthcoming meals. Flowers were placed on the table in the evening and a mixture of herbs brushed into the floor and also on the carpet square with a damp straw broom which would crush the essence of the herbs to relax the mind after a busy day. These herbs were not allowed to be crushed until just after four o'clock in the afternoon, after the pressure lamps had been pricked and primed ready to serve us with light for the evening meal. Their essence could release and remove the odor of kerosene without overpowering the men when they took off their boots and hats and had scrubbed up in preparation for the evening meal after the end of a long day in the paddocks.

The garden was all coordinated and grandmother planted the colors according to the colors of the rainbow. Herbs were sprinkled throughout as a companion to the flowers. You were introduced into the white flowers when you walked outside the door, its color cleared the cluttered mind and as you stepped forward you walked into the soft pinks; continuing down through the lilacs, into the blues of the cornflowers, then the greens which were the soft green of the Canterbury bells and onto the richer colors of lemons, oranges, reds and browns and as a child, it was like walking through a rainbow. My grandmother said that the colors were compatible with our inner alphabet as they urged us forward; our inner alphabet related to the words we would use, when we were busily thinking our thoughts. It was like an inner cleansing and healing of the chakras, as it is known today, back in my time it was known as Joseph's coat of many colors or the inner rainbow healing our self.

I knew how important each flower was by the color they emitted from the plant. You could read the value of the flower and what it had to offer you by the strength of its color. Even down to which part of the body it would be called to heal. The deeper the color, the more it connected to the problem in the lower section of the body. The lighter the color, the higher vibration was created. This is exactly the same as the colors we automatically release from our mind as we think each thought! We all have this inner rainbow that mathematically collects and arks its way up through our spinal column, when we think positive thoughts. These colors permeate their way throughout our aura, where they are reflected out to others.

Now you can understand the Biblical story of Joseph (remember, as mentioned in my other works that Joseph is decoded as 'Youseph'. The word Youseph interprets as 'yourself'—through the codes of the unconscious mind—higher mind and his coat of many colors!).

And in the center of grandmother's land was the rose garden. There was a large rectangle green lawn, bordered with around a hundred rose bushes, all coordinated of course. We would pose for photos in the rose gallery, whether it was an engagement, Christmas gathering, wedding, anniversary or someone's birthday party. It did not matter if the weather was hot or cold, there was always a section of the garden that we could stand in front of and pose! That is the nice thing about my country, there is always a flower in bloom all year long. We saved the washing up water after the dishes were done, the bath water after we had finished our scrub up, the washing water when the clothes had been hung up to dry—all collected and bucketed out on to the garden. The men in the family did all of the preparation work to the soil and when the earth was ready, it was up to the women to put in the cuttings and strew the seeds.

My grandmother cooked her scrumptious meals, full of fresh vegetables and herbs, which were always ground in the mortar and pestle that she had brought back from China in the beginning of the 1900's, where she had studied Chinese herbal medicine, and the art of painting on ceramics, plus food preparation for three years; her order of the day was little and often, feeds the man; as this is the Asian way, in which she was taught. This stimulates the alchemy of their brain where they are always walking ahead of themselves and not lagging behind.

She was always explaining herbs and spices that she learned about in China during the preparation of each meal. "Be careful of curry, don't rob the meal of its own flavor, it is there to enhance the meal and the spices are to retrain the lining of the stomach as well as feed the endocrine system, and then work its way through to the immune system", she would say. "Be very careful of chili, it is only to be used once a month, if then. Why do I tell you this? We speak the English language; you don't need to inflame or stimulate your ego into distancing itself from taking a step forward. It needs to keep within its own boundaries to allow your emotions and feelings to also take their place within your vocabulary. Chili disturbs the language we speak, where we have a tendency to become more abrupt and callous with our choice of words".

Through research, and the lessons learned from customers who came into our restaurant and wanted more chili in their meals, I quickly read their body language and realized that they were trapped in their thinking and were desperate to try and perpetuate their mind. Chili gave them that instant rush of cortisol which tied them over, (cortisol, the primary stress hormone, increases sugars—glucose, in the bloodstream, enhances the brain's use of glucose and increases the availability of substances that repair tissues). I discovered that the chemical elements in chili force the body to go beyond its normal comprehension, where it becomes addictive to the consumer through the ego's demands. Their tired and stressed voice is usually the first things we begin to notice, then to their own detriment, they become aggressive and quick to show their anger, as their overstressed ego tries to regain control over their thoughts in all situations and conversations. Due to the body's over production of cortisol, over time, people become lethargic and develop a weakened immune system. They will crave for more chili, as the mind of their ego becomes inflamed and reaches for a perpetual escape as their original thinking has been annulled, through the ego's vilification.

Chili is a plant of medication, to be used sparingly in healing. It lifts the layers of the stomach lining and distributes the toxins that are caught up in that area; all created through your repetitious thinking of an old thought or idea that has still not been digested correctly; those old thoughts have already served their purpose to you. Therefore, by you overdosing on chili there is no need to purge or permanently cleanse yourself of everything you have placed in your mouth. I noticed in hot countries if used sparingly, it is a healer to cool the body down when one becomes overheated and overloaded, where too many thoughts are running rampant with nowhere to reside as they have not let go of their past thinking. Now do you understand the haunting of old thoughts forced upon us by our own ego, as to how we create the diseases that occur in later life?

Please take a look at the countries that use chili in their hot and spicy meals; they are still at loggerheads with one another, as well as their neighbor next door. Why? They repress themselves when they cannot find contentment to their own inner sanctum. Their mind is measuring with other like mindedness, as they become deterred with their own thinking. This is the stage where they search for compatibility of thought, as they cannot find satisfaction within themselves; they feel that there is a part of themselves that are missing and on an unconscious level they connect to one another and automatically group together.

The latest information released, is the new research being conducted in relationship to chili and the connection to dementia, which is now affecting young people in their early twenties as their mind tries desperately to reshape itself. Fifty years ago, when I was taking an interest in the healing modalities, dementia began to awaken itself in the human chain as we moved into our late sixties, early seventies. How come we have brought the statistics down to the person who is only twenty years old? Another theory is the testing on chili and the new cancer strains that are mutating so quickly. What has drastically happened to our immune system, over such a short period of time, to disturb our thinking to such an extent?

Oh! The memories flood into my mind when I allow my memory bank to release its information. I have spoken of my grandmother's words in many seminars around the globe; of course, the chili addicts scoffed at my explanations. The parents and other siblings all agreed with me and were grateful for the information.

So, my grandmother was right; her Chinese education taught her to use chili sparingly and less often, to allow the stomach to clean itself naturally. Watch what you eat. Again, I ask you to relook at the countries that use this product for their own excuses, every day in the meal intake. And to end this section of my grandmother, before leaving China to migrate to Australia, she also studied Confucianism for a number of years, which continued right throughout her life. This information was passed down to the family as we grew into adult hood.

On a present note, one in ten babies born in my land, have allergies to food. We are number one in the world for allergies, and yet we have the healthiest fruit and vegetables that I have seen, as I travelled around the world. And yet so many have become allergic to this miracle. Why? Millions of dollars are spent in research to find an answer to this difficult situation.

An allergy is an immune system response or an over-reaction to the food you eat; or the animal you connect too. The same goes for the mold on the walls, dust mites, medication, insect bites and stings, to name a few. Now for the big one, an allergy is opened up on an inner level to react negatively through your thinking becoming blocked; all through you not expressing your desire to equate to the thought of your moment. You are busy designing, expressing an idea and not thinking it through to its completeness. This intolerance can be overcome much quicker through you finishing the ideas that are bouncing forward to be acknowledged, when you are in too much of a hurry to create a balance to your thinking.

Ninety percent of all illness created in the human body, is created through how you organize your thinking and bring each equation, which is a collection of thoughts on one subject, to a completion, not how you bring each idea together! There is only seven to ten percent created through hereditary conditioning.

Throughout the threading of our DNA the majority of us are implanted with every disease known to man. This threading becomes cross wired, when our inner energy cannot follow its own pathway. Each thought that has not earned its own satisfaction is constantly repeated over and over again, where it chokes up the neural highways to create a constant traffic jam.

What fascinated me more, was for me to understand as the years of study went by, that our food habits changed, as our intellect advanced to unfold itself. How did this occur? Our body communicates to itself every second of our existence, having the most amazing conversations with one another, if our mind is not chattering away through old thoughts constantly repeating themselves, we are able to hone in on the inner conversations, just as our thoughts combine with one another to form our sentences. As we stepped forward intellectually, our ego was quick to deny our new found grace; therefore we would again crave our old food habits, which automatically slowed us down.

Our old thinking patterns would come back to haunt us! We seemed to be living the same experiences over and over again, as our body could not make headway to comprehend these current new ideas. There was no harmonizing and balancing of our mind. This held our thinking at bay and made our new education harder for us to accept. The Guardian in charge of these thoughts is in the hands of the Pituitary Gland, as it assesses the value of each thought, through them continuing their communal growth. Hopefully this explains to you how our diseases have free reign over all thoughts, if we are constantly walking backwards on our self. Thank you for reading these paragraphs.

We had our own meat from the chickens, turkeys, ducks, and geese; then there were the sheep, pigs, wild goats and cattle. We could supply our own terrines, brawns, casseroles, pickled and smoked meats, roasts, milk, cream, butter and cheese. We had our own hives, which supplied our honey and assisted us in making our own candles with ground up lavender heads to rest our mind throughout the night. We had soap that could be used throughout the day, and a different blend for the night wash.

We planted our own orchards for fruit, jams and preserves, vegetables to share with our meals and chutneys and relishes. We baked our own bread, cakes and biscuits from the harvest of the wheat, oats, rice, millet, maize, and barley that we harvested each year.

We made our soap mixed with oats and lavender and calendula for the women to replace the moisture in our skin. Grandmother's knowledge of Aromatherapy was amazing as she explained the use of flowers owing to her training in China. There was ground up barley and softly sieved sand for the men to lift the grease off their hands as they washed them. These gifts from the eternal kingdom served us in many different ways. There were six meals per day, three large and three smaller ones. No one became ill, as our mind had been forewarned with our herbal concoctions.

Grandmother was also known as the local healer of the area. Her alchemy through the knowledge of herbs and spices were brilliant. There was no doctor in nearly a hundred and fifty kilometers and when someone in the area was sick, she would either receive a phone call or someone would come by the property and out she would go talking to her plants and gathering her herbs and her special big black cast iron pot would go on the old wood stove and the herbs were rendered down into a concoction of "one tablespoon a day please for seven days and then have three days off, to allow the body to catch up with the herbs and work on your illness." As a young child, my position in the house was to bless the bottles once they had come out of the sterilizer and sit alongside of her when she had poured the mixture in and make sure the cork was ready to place into the bottle. Of course, the people were healed in their given moment as they had turned their worries over to my grandmother. She always knew how strong their illness was and when to tell them to make an appointment in the nearest town to see the local doctor. And, sure enough they would go to town and have their operation, then come back to her for a checkup. I now know where I have inherited this information from. We don't follow in our parent's footsteps; we follow in the pathways our grandparents carved out for us to walk forward to inherit. As explained in my previous works, the ego tries to control the parent, and yet reveres the previous generation, which is released through a religious veneration that is generated through our mind and body balancing as a complete unit.

As the grapes that grew over the arbor at the rear of the house started to produce their new seasons growth, this helped keep the rooms cooler. Every child had to eat ten green grapes before they were ripe. This was to purify our blood and cleanse it after the short winter where we were rugged up all day. It worked! We were more than prepared for the long hot summer months ahead.

Grandmother never said "No! Don't touch." When I asked to rub a leaf together to emit the essence she would say, "yes, snip the fresh leaves cleanly from the top with your fingers, they are the freshest part of the plant and sniff the essence deep down into your lungs and anything nasty in the way of viruses, or pending diseases that is hanging around you looking for a place to reside and create itself, will soon leave home. Remember, we are all taught that God's gift to us is his garden." She also taught me how to plant my seeds with companion herbs. I learned the difference between herbs and weeds. A herb would benefit and a weed would hinder my flowers and vegetables. I learned to watch what weeds found their way forward into evolving their next evolutionary step, as they sprung up around my new seedlings, to see if they were a robber that would interfere with the energy of the new plant or if they were a friend which would form a relationship to strengthen the plant. The robber would feed itself on the innocence of the new growth; it was like a parasite and had to be removed.

Grandmother explained that the garden had much to teach us, as our body also worked on the same parallel as the garden. If we had thoughts that could not find their own strength, then there was a parasite that would create a nest for it to strengthen itself and a disease became immanent. My crops of vegetables were always successful. I learned to understand how the plant kingdom is identical to the human kingdom.

And we all know by now, that every species that has evolved on this planet, is indelibly imprinted and is mathematically registered within the genes of every human.

I now feel honored to finally understanding the magnificence to the language of the mathematical universal laws that every human must abide by. They are explaining how our genes communicate with one another to harmonize and balance our body; which prepares the mind for the words that autonomically release for us to speak. Who do I thank? I would like to thank God (when decoded it is explaining to us the **G**reatest **O**racle of the **D**ivine) which all belongs to our inner language, the one that keeps us on the straight and narrow, for anointing us with this genetic engineering which has become my most precious gift.

To return back to the story, my grandmother taught me back in the late-forties through to the mid-fifties, where and how to attract energy through planting the dried cow horns which were filled with their own waste products and buried, then months later were taken out of the ground and buried in the new garden bed. She also liked some of the cow horns to be filled with fresh sea sand once a year. When we had killed the beast, the horns were severed and placed on top of the ant nests; which were built up into mounds behind the toilet and this was half way down the paddock and a good three-minute walk away. I often wondered why the meat ants had collected to build their nests behind there. Anyway, the ants would clean the fibrous tissue out of the horns. We also used the cow horns as beakers to drink out of; flower vases on the table or cupboard, and they were lovingly polished with bee's wax where they glowed through the lamp light on the table.

It wasn't until the generators came out that we could enjoy the power of electricity with our 25-watt globes, which was only allowed for two hours of a night.

When members of the family would go for holidays to the ocean once a year after the wheat harvest, they had to bring back a fresh bucket of sand from the beach for grandmother. The silica and salt of the sand once buried inside the horns would change the molecular structure of the soil and no matter how tired or parched it felt, it would purify the soil and spring into life once again.

Grandmother having spent those three years in China in 1903-6, was taught how to hum to her vegetables and she would walk through her garden humming to her plants, which I now understand was creating a vibration firstly for the plants, as well as assisting her to reach her own resonance to promote her own sound. I can still recall how some of them seemed to bow to her as she walked down her rows. This fascinated me as there wasn't any wind to move them; they knew her sound and were honoring her.

We now understand that the symbol OM or AUM when chanted creates its own frequency, where we lift the eternal layers of consciousness to create a field of levitation which can occur, and my grandmother lived it around 140 years ago.

I can still recall the smell of the ocean when I put my head over the bucket as a child. It stayed fresh and never went sour and the smell was there all year long. There were millions of tiny little shells in the sand and these were ground up in the mortar and the pestle and grandmother would create them into a paste and this was scattered around certain plants who were not feeling too well. She explained to me that the shapes of these tiny shells were in perfect unison to God's original plan and that they would help to heal whatever they came into contact with. These old wives tales are still used as a reflection of today's intuitiveness, as they were all chemically free and correct at that time of our evolution. Today we have continued on with their story and advanced upon the knowledge of the past. Their mathematical shape would release the correct prescription to the plant. Today we are more aware of the spiral the golden mean creates as reflected in a sea shell.

Once again it was the men's job to collect the sand, as they had to make sure that it was not spilt on the way home, which was just on nine hundred kilometers away, over rough dirt roads. One memory that still abounds in my mind is that I can recall the thrill of driving on a bitumen road. The car seemed to glide over the road and I often stuck my head out of the car window to see if the tires were really on the road. I felt like we were flying as I could not feel the bumps of the corrugated dirt roads!

As my childhood expanded, I became fascinated with how things worked. I loved being outdoors; it was much safer than the kitchen. I had my own motorbike by the time I was nine. I learned to drive a semi-trailer from one gate to the next, when I celebrated my tenth birthday, I also received my first watch as I was now in double figures, therefore I had more responsibility to live up to and was to become more aware of time. I was propped up with wheat bags so that I could reach the brakes and accelerator with my father as the passenger guiding me through the gears. Another surprise was for my eleventh birthday when I received a 22 rifle with a box of shells that had to last me twelve months so there was not too much sky larking around. I could pull down a rabbit or two for the oven, but, if I took its life, I had to tell it a story of how it would benefit the family and thank it for its service to us.

I then had to skin and clean it myself and then I could take it into the kitchen, where it had to be soaked in coarse salt and water to clear the carcass of any toxins. I then had to place the pelt inside out on the u-shaped wire to dry and say thank you for the gift it had given me. As the pelts added up, they were sent to Sydney where they were tanned and made into the softest blankets one could imagine, we also made floor rugs and slippers, a small hat to keep our ears from chilblains and mittens to keep the hands and feet warm on cold and frosty mornings.

I could stop a goanna in his tracks as he was about to devour the eggs in the hen house or a snake who was about to devour the hens! The carcasses were dragged behind the toilet and placed on the ant's nest where in time we could view the skeletal structures bone by bone. My younger brother would compare them to the ancient prehistoric animals. No one bothered to stay in the toilet too long to read the scraps of paper, as the stench from the rotting carcass could be unbearable for a few days.

Another teaching of grandmother's was how to coil a piece of copper pipe and plant it into the ground; the end of the pipe had to be planted six inches into the ground to transfer the energy around the vegetable beds. She placed three copper coils around the rows in a triangle shape. It could not be four; that didn't work as four would divert the energy and could cancel itself out. Needless to say, we were again reminded that God's gift to us was in his garden.

I loved the stories she told, when she taught me all about the plant kingdom. That everything that God had designed had to earn its place on this planet. (Learning comes from explanations that we receive from someone else; earnings are released to us from your inner self). Every plant, every tree, all needed their own temperament to encourage them to grow, to advance themselves. They needed the minerals from under the earth and the elements in the earth to sustain them. Their territory became their boundary, they never ventured outside of their own perimeter, until the species of the planet assisted. Just as our own body needs the elements of the earth and minerals to keep us alive. Their seed could be carried along with the birds, the wind, the fire or the water, which propagated further down the track where they found a new home in soil of same mind. And that goes for every species on the planet as well; they have all had to earn their place to exist on the earth.

I can still recall some of her sayings when we were down in the mouth, "now remember, every cloud has a silver lining" or maybe it was "this too will pass" to assist us with what we were going through in the moment. If the same thought was still there the next morning, then we had held onto it for too long to support us, therefore we were hindering our own growth. As I write these words to you now, there are so many stories waiting to be shared with you. One that has stood by me all of my life was 'Aim for the highest; there is room at the top.' And as always after our church service had finished on Sundays, she would remind us children that at the end of our day there had to be something that we had learned to carry us forward into tomorrow and if we felt we had earned something, it would support us for the rest of our life! Do not allow your mind to keep on repeating its thoughts. If we had learned nothing, then we had totally wasted our day!! We all remember that message to this day.

This was my life as a child. And of course, I carried these teachings into my life as a married woman and passed them onto my children. Now it's the grandchildren's time and the great grandchildren's turn. If I was shaped like a phone or an iPad and had a keypad, maybe I would be heard more clearly!

Please have a long glass of water after reading this chapter, you have earned the cleanse. Thank you for listening to my story.

Excerpt from the book:
"Decoding The Laws Of The Universe",
Chapter One. Our Individual Universal Law
And The Laws Of The Universe, O.M. Kelly.

***

CHAPTER ONE
Our Individual Universal Law And The Laws Of The Universe

Introducing our Individual Universal Law and the Laws of the Universe.

It is our own Individual Universal Law creating the Laws of the Universe! It is where we all become involved, and, through time and cause and effect, we have created and advanced our evolution for all humanity to inherit. The Laws of the Universe, (also known as the Universal Law, the God essence and other terminology), is the Soul Energy of the Collective Consciousness; it is a mathematical program of all that is.

It is the Soul's purpose (each person) to be here on the planet, and each Soul must release and improve the energy that has collected from the past. We are asked to live and discover this inner truth that is embedded in the depths of the Laws of the Universe, which are embedded in each one of your cells. We have evolved for a very special reason.

Our own Individual Universal Law refers to the Metaphysical philosophy that each individual is responsible for creating their own reality through their thoughts and emotional intelligence. The nature of each person's thinking, unique perspective and energy contributes to the overall consciousness of the universe. This knowledge is transformative on a personal level; once we understand, we can make great waves for all of humanity to inherit.

OVERVIEW:

Our Individual Universal Law

We are each our own Universe with our own Individual Universal Law, and we exist within a greater Universe that has its own proprietary law as well.

You are your own Universal Law; and, as you think, so, too, you create. You are given this gift to be in charge of how your thoughts create your world. As you allow one thought to finish itself, the next one is waiting to release itself to you. Your next thought will wait patiently until you are silent enough to allow it to come through.

Your Individual Universal Law is not created by what you do, but, rather, by your silent thoughts, regressions (thinking in the past), joys, frustrations, and peace. It is the energy and evolution of your emotional intelligence and how you connect to you.

Once you understand what your Individual Universal Law is, keep yourself focused, and you will be able to fulfil all your desires. Life will bring you up, through the temperance of your Soul, and, when you can define this inner education, you will become the Divine.

The Laws of the Universe

It is our Individual Universal Law creating the Laws of the Universe! It is where we all become involved, and, through time and cause and effect, we have created and advanced our evolution for all humanity to inherit. These Laws of the Universe are also known as the following: Collective Consciousness, Universal Law, the God essence, Collective Library of the Consciousness, World Consciousness, Collective Inheritance, Collective Memory, Collective Mind, Collective Soul of the God Force, Akashic Hall of Records, Hall of Recognition, Soul Energy of Collective Consciousness, and other terminology.

The Laws of the Universe (Collective Consciousness) registers all our conscious thinking, which must return to the conscious mind in order for our energy to continue to grow through the human evolution. The past is still alive in the Collective

Consciousness; that Collective Inheritance is all of our thinking and evolution. We cannot forget yesterday, but we can absorb it; we can soak it up into our own consciousness and use it in the moment.

The Laws of the Universe answers to our thinking in a balanced way, but it is not always in the way that we expect it to be! Another name for it is Karma, or the "Kha-Rha-Mha", if we explain it correctly, for this goes back to the early language of the Armenians and the hieroglyphs of Egypt. If we pronounce it in its correctness, it is the cause and effect, or the accidental and occidental; it is the occidental that is the key to your wisdom. The occidental is the final outcome of the length of your stay on this planet. The occidental is the light that keeps this planet alive.

So, your knowledge of these secrets can carry you to the place where you have the opportunity to dance along with these Laws of the Universe.

As you begin to believe in yourself, your Soul (your Soul is your life force) gives you never-ending gifts of knowledge. To believe in yourself takes a tremendous amount of courage, and that courage will lead you into other parallel worlds of existence. Those worlds align within and open you up to your inner worlds, and then you have earned the freedom to use them to promote your tomorrows.

EXPLAINED FURTHER—DELVING DEEPER:

<u>Our Individual Universal Law</u>

Let us explore further, our own Individual Universal Law. As stated previously your Individual Universal Law is not created by what you do, but, rather, by your silent thoughts, regressions (thinking in the past), joys, frustrations, and peace. It is the energy and evolution of your emotional intelligence and how you connect to you.

Understanding and connecting with our emotional intelligence is key to tapping into our Individual Universal Law. This involves becoming aware of our thoughts, of our emotions, learning to identify and process them, and understanding the ways in which they influence our actions, and outcomes we experience in life. By paying attention to the patterns and themes that emerge in our lives, we can begin to identify the underlying beliefs and values that shape our perceptions of reality.

Our emotional intelligence is instrumental to the evolution of our Individual Universal Law. Our emotions are energy in motion, and they have a vibrational frequency that attracts experiences and circumstances of a similar frequency. When we are in a positive emotional state, we are vibrating at a higher frequency, and we tend to attract positive experiences and people into our lives. Conversely, when we are in a negative emotional state, we are vibrating at a lower frequency, and we tend to attract negative experiences and people into our lives.

Therefore, to evolve our Individual Universal Law and attract more positive experiences into our lives, it is crucial to work on our emotional intelligence and maintain a positive emotional state as much as possible. This means being aware of our emotions, expressing them in healthy ways, and choosing to focus on positive emotions such as love, gratitude, joy, and a feeling of peace with oneself. We can use mindfulness, staying in the moment and have an awareness of the chatter of the mind.

We can also examine your "relationship of self". Your relationship of self is the way you relate to you. It is created by the thoughts you have about yourself, belief in self, the emotions you feel in regards to yourself, your judgements about yourself, your perception your self-worthiness and how you honour yourself—and the big one, your internal dialogue to self. When your belief in self builds upon its own strength and creates your next positive thought, your life becomes so much easier for you to manage.

How can we improve our relationship with ourselves, and what steps can we take to cultivate a more positive internal dialogue that supports our self-belief and self-worth? How can we break free from negative thought patterns and judgments about ourselves, and build a stronger foundation of self-love and self-acceptance that empowers us to create a more fulfilling life? How can we identify and change limiting beliefs that may be holding us back, and replace them with more empowering beliefs that support our growth and development? The answer is by cultivating a positive internal dialogue. Improving our relationship with ourselves involves several steps. Firstly, we need to become aware of our current internal dialogue and how we talk to ourselves. We can start by observing our thoughts and emotions, and noticing any patterns of negativity or self-judgment. Once we have identified these patterns, we can work on changing them by replacing negative self-talk with positive self-talk and affirmations of "I believe in myself". To cultivate a more positive internal dialogue, we can furthermore practice self-compassion and self-forgiveness. To break free from limiting beliefs and judgments about ourselves, we can challenge these beliefs and reframe them in a more positive and empowering light. This can involve seeking out new perspectives and information, and exploring new ways of thinking and being. When your belief in self builds upon its own strength and creates your next positive thought, watch how the miracles manifest in your life where you will find you are continuously working as one with the universe.

This journey is yours and cannot be given to anyone else; the responsibility is yours alone. The hierarchical mind/unconscious mind/higher mind, also known as the Higher Self, will always be there to step in front of you, protecting and holding you firmly when you cannot believe or when you have lost your trust in you. Our Higher Self is a deeper and evolved aspect of our being and has access to higher levels of wisdom, intuition, and guidance. Our Higher Self, presents experiences for us. It gives us the opportunity for our thoughts to repeat throughout our life until we can find the strength to overcome them. This suggests that our Higher Self may be trying to teach us something or help us grow by presenting recurring negative thoughts, experiences, or fears.

Our thinking can create our fear in the moment by the way we perceive and interpret our experiences. Our thoughts and beliefs about a situation can trigger a fear response in our body, even if there is no actual physical threat. Our thoughts can also create a negative feedback loop, where the fear response reinforces the negative thinking, leading to more fear and anxiety. By changing our thinking and challenging our beliefs, we can break this cycle and reduce our fear and anxiety in the moment.

If you find yourself repeatedly experiencing negative thoughts, fears, or experiences, it is important to stop them before they become greater. Remember the traffic lessons you learned in school: stop, look, and listen. Take a moment to search beyond the present moment and see how this energy or thought is recreating itself. To search beyond the present moment, is to take a step back and analyse the situation objectively. One way to do this is to observe the thoughts and feelings that arise when the negative thought, experience or fear resurfaces. Ask yourself questions such as: What triggered this thought or feeling? What emotions am I experiencing? Is there a pattern to these thoughts and feelings? Reflect on how this thought or fear has impacted your life and try to gain insight into why it keeps coming back. This process of self-reflection can help you identify the underlying causes of the negative thought or fear and find ways to overcome it. This is not a learning experience, but an earning experience. The difference between the two is that learning means "looking at" something, while earning means "looking through" it. Your Higher Self, presents these experiences to you as an opportunity to overcome them. One thing in life is certain: You cannot run away from yourself. There is nowhere to hide! You create your fear in the moment through your thinking. Write this down: "My fear is created by me, as I am refusing to live and accept this Divine moment in my life." By acknowledging your power over your thoughts, you can take the first step towards personal transformation. If I can help you to understand and accept, where you can act out your thoughts through self-confidence and assurance; and then we are both winners. Hopefully you will have the opportunity to rake away your fears, as this is the sole—and Soul—reason for you to be here, and it is what this life's quest is all about. We rake up all the leaves after the autumn season has ended, and we prepare the garden for winter. Winter is the time for hibernation, and it is through our own hibernation that we are given the time to dichotomize, which means to sort out right from wrong and refrain from making the same mistakes. When we look out our window again, our garden looks tidy and free; the raking has allowed it to regain its own silence and to breathe new life as it prepares to birth itself for the next season.

For years in the journey to discover this metaphysical knowledge (that is, before I became an Adept in the Secrets), I went into the "Worlds of Invisible Kingdoms" (explored other dimensions) and was asked by my teachers to read the Bible in the reverse from Revelations back to Genesis, instead of the other way around. It is not necessary for you to do this. My teachers informed me that, by doing this, I could bring through a resonance of intelligence that all of humanity could view from within themselves—where they could understand the capabilities of how their intelligence unfolds itself, and then that knowledge would be available for them to add to what they had already achieved. "Why?" I asked my teachers. "Your program fits the bill" they told me. "What program?" I persisted. "The thoughts of your previous generations have been indelibly imprinted in you, and you have made yourself available; you asked, so now you have the opportunity to receive!" That's what they told me!

To further explain, a "life program". Your life program was created through your parents' DNA, which provided the basic principles for you to become you. Your task is to unfold yourself through the disadvantages of your parents' judgment and (mis)understanding themselves! You have chosen to live what your parents were too afraid to face through their acceptance of self as they understood it, and, more importantly, you have also chosen to live their gains.

Your life program keeps on creating itself through each of your thoughts building upon the other, and the transformation continues until you have taken your last breath. That energy force field grows in strength and opens you up into your Higher—or heavenly—Self. That Higher Self follows you through every thought you think, always encouraging you to create and expand your thinking.

To carry your DNA inheritance into your next step of humanity's earnings is how and why you have evolved to be here, through balancing and clearing your past generations' thinking and programming the basics of the mind of your future generations. Once you have accepted this program, it is no longer a detriment to your consciousness; the freedom you create in your mind will allow your intelligence to have the ability to evolve even further. Once we have recognized and solved the tasks that have been given to us by our genetic inheritance, we are free to collect more information to add to the benefits available to us beyond this program.

During those years of my internal searching, my intelligence grew into the "Wisdom of the Sages", where I could see through the layers of restriction that I had hidden behind for my own protection. I also began to study the science behind humanity's thinking, and, as this information grew, understanding it fully became my ultimate goal; as a result, over the years, all knowledge consumed me. I found I could unite the plumber with the librarian, the lawyer with the builder, the electrician with the social worker, and then unite them all into a whole! It is the relationship of self that connects us to the energy of our total evolution. This knowledge has grown stronger and stronger over the last thirty years of my life. Subsequently, I brought all this information into a format that is ongoing in every moment of my life. I learned how to transfer this knowledge into the human body by beginning with just one cell.

Once you understand what your Individual Universal Law is, keep yourself focused, and you will be able to fulfil all your desires. To keep ourselves focused and fulfil our desires according to our Individual Universal Law, we need to maintain a clear and positive mindset. This means consistently monitoring our thoughts and redirecting any negative or limiting beliefs towards positive and empowering ones. We can do this by practicing mindfulness and being present in the moment, observing our thoughts and choosing to let go of any that do not serve us. Visualization and affirmations can also be powerful tools to help us stay focused and aligned with our desired outcomes. By visualizing ourselves already having achieved our goals and repeating positive affirmations that affirm our abilities and worthiness to receive what we desire, we can tap into the power of our Higher Self and attract more of what we want into our lives. Life will bring you up, through the temperance of your Soul, and, when you can define this inner education, you will become the Divine.

The Laws of the Universe

Let us explore further The Laws of the Universe. As stated, it is our Individual Universal Law creating the Laws of the Universe! It is where we all become involved, and, through time and cause and effect, we have created and advanced our evolution for all humanity to inherit. The Laws of the Universe (Collective Consciousness) registers all our conscious thinking, which must return to the conscious mind in order for our energy to continue to grow through the human evolution. The past is still alive in the Collective Consciousness; that Collective Inheritance is all of our thinking and evolution. We cannot forget yesterday, but we can absorb it; we can soak it up into our own consciousness and use it in the moment.

The Collective Consciousness registers all our conscious thinking by storing and recording every thought, emotion, and experience in a universal database or energy field. It is the energy of the thought, emotion, and experience that registers with the Collective Consciousness on a quantum level. Basically explained on a quantum level, our thought energy interacts with the universe through the observer effect. This effect describes how the act of observation can change the behaviour of particles and systems in the universe. When we focus our thoughts on something, we are essentially observing it with our consciousness, and this observation can affect the behaviour of particles and systems related to that thing. According to quantum physics, all particles and systems in the universe are interconnected and entangled. This means that our thoughts and intentions can have an impact on the behaviour of these interconnected particles and systems. Our thoughts and emotions emit energy waves that can influence the energy of the Laws of the Universe, the Collective Consciousness. (The physical particle-like structure of matter existing in time-space, in which it exists non-locally "encoded" as a wave frequency in the past, present and future of the Collective Consciousness—the holographic universe).

This collective inheritance of knowledge and wisdom is available to us all and can be tapped into for personal growth and evolution. (Time-space reality is the frequency domain of the Higher Mind as well as the Collective Consciousness). As individuals contribute their thoughts and experiences to the collective, the database expands and evolves, contributing to the evolution of humanity as a whole.

As previously mentioned, The Laws of the Universe answers to our thinking in a balanced way, but it is not always in the way that we expect it to be! Another name for it is Karma, or the "Kha-Rha-Mha", if we explain it correctly, for this goes back to the early language of the Armenians and the hieroglyphs of Egypt. If we pronounce it in its correctness, it is the cause and effect, or the accidental and occidental. It is the occidental that is the key to your wisdom. The occidental is the final outcome of the length of your stay on this planet. The occidental is the light that keeps this planet alive. That gift from the All That Is, is our attainment, and it is also how we have produced our next moment. Weather patterns, diseases, viruses, and wars are all creations of the atmospheric conditions of the Collective Consciousness; they are the results of the thinking of this planet. Our accidents are what we have produced for ourselves through our thinking. The occidental is the explanation, as to how we have gathered and achieved the accident in the first place. It is not only what you have done to you; it is how the Laws of the Universe answer back to what you are doing to you. I like to refer to the occidental as the "messenger" represented as the Pigeon throughout the Laws of Shamanism. With its sonic sound, it homes in on a catastrophic conclusion of thought, and then it delivers the message to our heavenly home, which is our brain.

A BRIEF METAPHYSICAL OVERVIEW OF THE BRAIN/MIND

A brief description of the structure of our brain/mind (a metaphysical interpretation): Our brain has two sides. The left brain is our logic (conscious mind). The left brain is our masculine side; our ego, our primal fear, and as stated our logic. It represents how we are representing ourselves to others through releasing from within. The right brain is our emotions (subconscious mind). The right brain is our feminine side, our inner creativity. We give out to others with the right side, and our energy in motion—or emotion—creates itself from how we are giving and receiving to and from the self. The right brain represents what we are doing to ourselves within, and what we are capable of receiving through ourselves–through our being aware of that giving.

The people who live in their logical ego sense are perfect, and so, too, are the people who live in their creative emotional sense. In understanding the logical sense, we understand through our primal inheritance, where it begins to fit with common sense. The mind of logic is the echo from whatever is created, and it is also what we attract in our outer worlds; the emotional mind sits within and takes care of our sense of responsibility.

We cannot survive on this planet without both ego and emotions. Our journey is to learn how to balance both brains so that we may become aware of the supportiveness of our unconscious mind/higher mind. The unconscious/higher mind, also known as our Soul/Higher Self, is the freedom with which we can tune into understanding ourselves, but only when the other two have balanced through our attitude to our self. We touch and connect to our unconscious mind/higher mind, as the other two brains encompass the Soul through looking into one another.

If we like to take this further; our left brain, our conscious self, is responsible for the first and second-dimensional mind. Our right brain, our subconscious self; is responsible for the third dimension and the relationship to the introduction of the fourth dimension. The balance of both brains is the doorway up into our unconscious mind/higher mind, which allows it to be responsible for the temple of self to live up to its expectations. Through balancing your mind, you uplift your emotions, and you become not only more aware of your intelligence but also more emotionally aware. This emotional intelligence is a reasoning of perpetual motion, which continuously balances and harmonizes your mind, body, and Soul, and which also equates to your family, friends, and country. The whole planet has the opportunity of continually harmonizing and reflecting itself back to you, and this reflection is the mind, body, and Soul of all.

Temple of self relates to the training of our self, moment by moment, where we learn to have a deeper understanding as to how we balance and control our thinking. It is where we earn the right to be in control of the incessant chattering that the ego likes to try to regain and re-control every situation as it did before! Our unconscious/higher mind is the make-up of our Divine Inheritance—or the language of our Soul—it is our life force. The unconscious mind/higher mind is the world of telepathic communication that every person tunes into on an etheric level, whether they believe in it or not. It is the ultimate reason you are here experiencing your life's journey.

***

I wrote my books for you, not your friends or family. The purpose of my work is to explain, in written form, the quest of your own intelligence, where you will realize that you have no limits as to discovering your outer boundaries. I would like you to learn how to understand yourself first. Only through understanding yourself do you have the opportunity to nourish and nurture others. Allow your family and friends the opportunity to make their own mistakes, and they will then learn to earn their own gains. Through understanding this message, you are conforming through a state of Grace. On my journey I discovered in my reading research it was the little things such as in Galatians 5:1: "Stand fast therefore in the liberty wherewith Christ hath made us free, and be not entangled again with the yoke of bondage." Which means, do not become entangled with your fear to the point where your own restrictions bind you. I discovered thousands of verses like this, and they helped me release the pressures of my past's hold on me—at last, through my awareness, I could see how my past tried to control me, but I also saw how to watch it surrender as it grew steadfast within itself!

Another little verse that gave me sustenance throughout the journey was from the Book of Thomas in verse 2—which is one of my favourites, as it reveals many answers—this verse is about the words spoken by Jesus: "Let him who seeks continue seeking until he finds. When he finds, he will become troubled, he will be astonished through his own revelations, and he will rule over the all." This passage explains the search for self. Once we have suffered enough through not being able to understand ourselves our fear immediately jumps to attention—simply because it has no other direction to take. We become troubled when we cannot see or hear our next step. These words were a great revelation to me as I fumbled and stumbled along.

Read on, and the Universe will return to you all the answers that you need to unfold your truth.

Excerpt from the book:
"Decoding Sacred Fung Shwa", Chapter One.
The Meaning Of Sacred Fung Shwa, O.M. Kelly.

***

CHAPTER ONE
The Meaning Of Sacred Fung Shwa

Your house is your home, which is an exemplified creation of the Place or Palace where you call home and live in, as it is in service to you. Moreover, it is a representation of your emotional intelligence, revealing aspects of your inner self to others. When visitors enter your home, they unconsciously read this energy shaping their perception of how you value and honour yourself.

Chinese Feng Shui divides the world into five elements: wood, fire, earth, metal and water. With Sacred Fung Shwa, I have introduced a Metaphysical sixth element "Your Life Force". My interpretation is the next step towards the evolution of how we can understand, with more substantiation, the evolution that releases back to us through the principles of the unconscious/higher mind. The Chinese already know and have accepted what we, in the Western world, are now just beginning to learn and understand. Fung Shwa is a form of energy that comes from within. The "Fung" is the sound, and the "Shwa" is the result of that sound. For example, a clap means "attention!"; the sound that the clap makes, is the Fung returning to self, and the vibration that comes from the clap is the Shwa – the Shwa is the result of the Fung. Each time I clap my hands, that clap is a symbol of the relationship between you and me, and this vibration allows me to hold your attention. When we hold our attention, we are focused and waiting in anticipation for the next movement.

To further explain, Fung Shwa energy comes from within; it is the same as our life force. In Feng Shui, the life force is referred to as "Chi", which is the energy that flows through everything in the universe, including human beings. In some cultures, the life force of the universe is called "Chi", "Prana", or "Mana", while others refer to it as the "Force", "Universal Energy" or "Life Energy". Regardless of the name, this energy is the driving force behind all things. The universe is full of energy and life. Every single thing in the universe is made up of energy, including humans, animals, and even inanimate objects. This energy is called the life force of the universe. The life force of the universe is the energy that flows through everything, connecting all things in existence. This energy is the source of all life and creation, and it is responsible for the movement, growth, and evolution of everything. The life force of the universe is not limited by time or space. It exists everywhere and at all times, flowing through the universe reminiscent of an endless river. By learning to connect with and harness this energy, we can tap into the infinite potential of the universe and create a life full of abundance and fulfilment.

This energy is the source of all life and creation, which is responsible for the movement, growth, and evolution of everything. The life force of the universe is not limited by time or space. It exists everywhere and at all times, flowing through the universe reminiscent of an endless river through to the smallest brook. It finds its own strength through climbing over rocks, sliding down embankments, picking up its own speed and knows how and where to calm itself when its own pressure becomes entangled. By learning to connect with and through harnessing this energy, we can tap into the infinite potential of the universe and create a life full of abundance and fulfilment.

The life force of a human being is also known as "Chi" or "Qi" in traditional Chinese culture. It is the vital energy that flows through the body and keeps us alive. This energy flows through channels in the body called meridians. Chi is not just limited to physical health, but also affects a person's emotional and mental well-being. When chi flows freely, a person is in good health and balance. However, when the flow of chi is blocked, a person may experience physical, emotional, or mental imbalances, which can manifest as pain, illness, or emotional distress. In a Metaphysical interpretation, your Soul is your life force (your life's energy), your energy is your force field, and your force field is your aura, (the aura is the energy that is produced within your cells). Your Soul is the energy that collects from your unconscious/higher mind. Your Soul's journey is through the vibrational energy that releases through your heart, from your thoughts, which alerts the brain – whether that be positive or negative energy. This is your life force.

Fung Shwa is where we bring every aspect of our energetic light (life force) into the oneness, through the balancing of the mind, which you create in the moment. Being "in the light" means that you are forming a web – or net – of your own consciousness up into the Collective Consciousness, which through its positive behaviour relays all around the planet. Each time you think a thought in your truth, that thought attracts attention; somebody out there waits for the support of that thought. This is how the feldic (from the German word "Feld", which means "field") grid forms around the planet.

With every thought you think, you are permanently reaching out and bringing your future to you; so accept that you are the Fung! The energy of your Shwa is collected and stored in your unconscious/higher mind, not in your conscious (ego) or subconscious (emotional) minds. As we collect a thought to think, we create a vibration of energy that is collected up into the storehouse of the unconscious/higher mind, where the results are the Shwa!

Karma – or "Kha-Rha-Mha" – is the Shwa of the Fung; it is the result of your action. The more centred you become through this adjustment, the more you influence your house or your workplace; this places an added responsibility onto the whole planet, asking humanity to rearrange the thinking of the Collective Consciousness. As it is representing a higher form or level of communication.

The Chinese communicate with one another through a wonderful world of symbolism. Their alphabet is pictographic (closer to ancient cuneiform than to Western phonetic alphabet systems), and its symbolic structure is based on the Fibonacci sequence, which is collected mathematically through the golden mean. They have introduced us to a picture within a picture.

Whilst in China with a group of my students, a professor who was introducing us into their language asked for my country of birth. After I told him that I was from Australia, he proceeded to draw the character of Australia. Through that character, he was also explaining that I lived across the sea to the south, in a land of sunshine and vastness, a land of colour and brightness. I became quite homesick by the time he was finished regaling my homeland, which I had not seen for a number of years. That symbol did not only describe the word "Australia", it also created a picture that explained where the land was situated, where I was from, and what the country looked like – the small picture was so complete that no further explanations were necessary. This information is similar to how the Australian Aboriginals create their paintings as they place themselves up into their own royal behaviour, which is similar to how we prepare our mind as we collect ourselves for meditation. This empowerment releases them from the strength of their ego where they can easily slip into a state of grace and conformity to lift their mind above the earth, as their paintings are always looking down from a greater height, reminiscent of a drone.

Excerpt from the book:
"Power Thought For The Day Oracle Book",
Introduction, How to Use The Book,
15. Dolphin—Free Will,
16. Whale—Conversation and Communication,
O.M. Kelly.

***

POWER THOUGHT FOR THE DAY ORACLE BOOK
A Metaphysical Interpretation

You are and have always been
the greatest gift to the earth.

Each species that has evolved on this planet is recorded in our cellular memory. Our thinking began with the world of Trees, where we yearned to stand upright. In the form of the human body, the tree species are embedded in the feet and lower legs. The tree's opposite was attracted and became the worm. The worm came out of the oceans of consciousness to invest in the ground where its strength grew through the importance of self, and then it evolved into the serpent, where it took its place above the ground.

The Animal Kingdom then took its place in our evolution where we learned to understand ourselves, and this understanding became the collective of our left brain. We released our tail and our rudder disappeared; our sole responsibility was passed down to us in order for us to steer our own vessel in the direction that we wished to travel. The taller we stood the more our consciousness expanded towards the heavens. This second collection of evolution is situated from the knees to the navel.

The next step up the evolutionary ladder presented itself to us through the Bird Kingdom, which is collected and gathered from the navel to the heart. We begin to earn the strength of our heart when we enter into this Kingdom, through entering into and opening up our right brain. These are the worlds of our emotions or our 'energy in motion'. We have evolved and grown through our confidence, trusting and believing in itself.

From the heart we move up into the chest area to the throat, which creates the third section and this is the evolution of the ocean. The species of the oceans help us to release the intelligence of the unconscious mind (higher mind), the hidden mind; the one that we cannot see. It silently works on our behalf showing us our flaws through the injustices that we return to ourselves; we receive these thoughts through our vision world. We began to recognise this when we conceived of the word 'imagination' which, in our innocence we refer to as our dreams.

From the throat or the base of the brain we enter into the unconscious mind (higher mind) and this is the world of the insect. The insect has evolved to reduce and replace the irritations to the exalted mind. From here we have the power to hone into the potentiality of our sonar or sonic sound, which is the design of the inner ear, to correct the 'mathematics'; of the conscious and subconscious minds which, when understood correctly, are the worlds of the extra-terrestrial.

Insects rely on their sonar, as they do not eat matter; they remove and digest only the juices. They represent the alchemy that we produce in the brain; these are resonances that we collate through the two holes in the roof of our mouth.

Now let us hear the above story again on a metaphysical observation: As the tree grows, it moves up and throughout our system. The animal becomes our ego. The bird evolution lifts us up into our angelic nature through the opening of the heart, where we offer to return our favours to others.

Then we move deeper into the collective consciousness of the ocean and we enter into the worlds of our unconscious mind (higher mind). This section of the brain is much greater in matter and holds limitless opportunities to benefit our future. The more we accept our own future. The more we accept our own intellect; the more we add to what we can achieve. This is the fourth dimension appearing into our psyche and it presents the opportunity for us to accept responsibility for the consequences that are delivered back to us through our higher mind. This is the world of cause and effect.

We now enter into the next evolution of humanity as the human brain begins to reinvest in itself. The layers of the Pia Mater (the piousness of self), the Arachnoid (the gathering of the web we weave) and the Dura Mater (the durability of self) are the three membranes that cover both hemispheres of the brain and the spinal cord. These membranes thicken and strengthen this outer perimeter and through time these layers will magnify holographically and lead the way for us to offer greater expectations to self.

Each step of evolution is opening us up to extra responsibilities of self and as we move forward we must accept the reasoning as to why they evolved in the first place. For you to progress in your mind, the old thoughts that you have hung onto for security must automatically release and diminish. The old story is repeatedly handed down to us with each generation. We must overtake the past generation knowledge and gain mastery of our own divine wisdom; otherwise the story is repeatedly creating the same mistakes over and over again.

We are now aware that the extinction of the Animal Kingdom could easily be an effect of human cause. We have overtaken their reasoning as to how and why they evolved in the first place. They now form the make-up of our second dimensional mind. We, as humans, must now accept our responsibility for the evolution of our animal species.

The dimensions presented in this introduction are the four directions that release you from your DNA. Each direction: North, South, East and West, is an evolutionary step of advancement into your acceptance of the responsibility of realising the potentiality of the alchemy that you control with your brain.

Through the 'Totem' energy of all, the ancient species that we have evolved before us, represent an emotional inheritance that we can rely on to sustain our moment. They will become the beneficial advisers to help us with our own intelligence when our mind is in the field of doubt.

HOW TO USE THE BOOK

Reality has no time; it is created through the 'mathematical form' that you have always relied on; reality is perceived to the level of your current intellect. Our higher mind has no time; it steps into and works on behalf of the thought of the moment. This book encompasses 22 Major Totem Power representations, symbolic of our evolution. Close your eyes and inhale and exhale a deep breath and relax and allow yourself no thought as you select the right page of the Shamanic animal presented in this book. The right page will always appear for you at the right moment and you will discover how the power animals are working with you for insight into their wisdom. Different power animals come into our lives at various phases offering messages to guide us on our path.

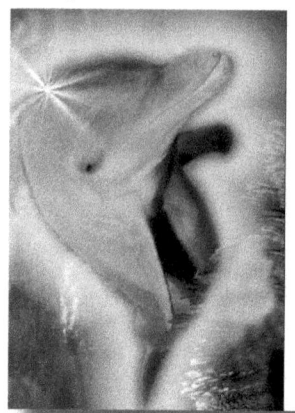

Images are in full colour in the book.

15.   DOLPHIN—Fee Will

You have chosen Dolphin because the Collective Consciousness has an important direction for you to follow throughout today. Allow your thoughts to become free from entanglement, and watch as you release the power to collect a greater substance to your knowledge, which will create new skills that you can tap into and benefit from. A focused mind can create on your behalf.

Dolphin is the teenager of consciousness; the young warrior who is out there to win in any situation and who requires a harmonious mind in order to do so. They can empower their energy to suit any situation by opening themselves up to attracting the collective inheritance.

You have the ability to apply your energy at the same speed as others who are in your presence. When a Dolphin swims beside a fast-moving ship, the Dolphin uses the power—or the energy—of that ship to add to its own energy in order to propel its motivational expertise through the water. That also explains to us the understanding of free will. The thrust, which comes through the belief of its own empowerment, can keep the Dolphin's speed equal to the speed of the ship, where the Dolphin then has the opportunity to power beyond the ship, through surging into its own free domain—if it so chooses. It is as if an astral restaurant is supplying the Dolphin with nourishment from that energy. Free will is the teenager, and it is also the warrior earning his wisdom through achieving his own self-will.

Enjoy your moments today and allow them to multiply through the freedom you have so richly earned. The dolphin empowers his mind through his desire for his outer world to be as exuberant as he feels on an inner level.
***

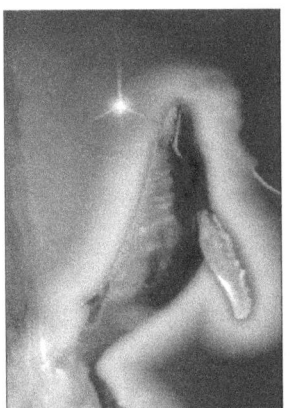

Images are in full colour in the book.

16.   WHALE—Conversation and Communication

Whales represent the intelligence of conversation and communication. When Whale enters your life the message is to keep your thoughts clear and precise, as they resonate unconsciously to all who surround you. Remember you are solely responsible for everything you say and do. Choose your words eloquently and Whale will support you in communicating clearly.

The Whale, in Shamanism, is the evolution of the word 'communication'. It represents the conversation, pulse, and tone throughout the Collective Consciousness, and it sends and receives sound only through that sonic level. The Whale's Spiritual awareness becomes the 'essence' that pronounces its own intellectual energy back to itself.

Whales create fields of light energy that can be seen from great distances, even from satellites travelling in the outer Universe. That vibration collects, and then it is forced through the next field of energy until it completes a full circuit. Whales can hear each other's thoughts through the sonic sound that they produce, through the beat of their own heart. The whale can communicate to every other whale in the ocean at the same time. Their sonic sound waves are carried throughout the Collective Consciousness and lived by its entire species simultaneously. Their sound waves are collected and carried along the ocean floor. All species that vibrate to the same frequency can hear and understand this sonic sound.

Whales live totally on the vibrations of the higher mind. This is the highest format of the mind, which we refer to as the "Royal Behaviour of Self'. The Whale moves slowly and thoroughly through the deliberation it has already inherited from the Collective Inheritance.

Books By O.M. Kelly (Omni)

Decoding The Mind Of God

Author O.M. Kelly's seminal work, "Decoding the Mind of God", is a compilation of nine volumes of metaphysical information based on the research into the coded information of the Laws of the Universe, also known as the Collective Consciousness, and represents a groundbreaking contribution to our understanding of the metaphysical universe. Now, all nine volumes are being released as separate, revised books, each offering a unique perspective on the universe's workings. Omni's work has been widely acclaimed for its depth of insight, and her contributions to the field of metaphysics have been groundbreaking.

The nine separate volumes encompassing:

The Laws of the Universe
Thought
Dis-Ease
Death
Sexuality and Spirituality
The Dolphin's Breath
Sacred Alphabet and Numerology
Sacred Fung Shwa
Extra-Terrestrial Intelligence.

Updated version of each book now being released separately.

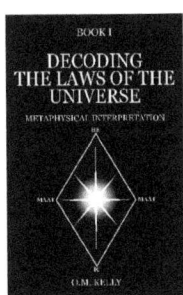

Book I. Decoding The Laws Of The Universe

If you're looking to unlock the hidden potential within you and transform your life, "Decoding the Laws of the Universe" is the book for you. This powerful and insightful book is designed to help you understand the deeper, metaphysical aspects of life and tap into the transformative power of the universe utilising the secrets of our Individual Universal Law.

This book serves to introduce you into the secrets of our Individual Universal Law. This amazing knowledge and wisdom, is transformative on a personal level and creates the opportunity for you to interrelate with the Laws of the Universe. Throughout this book, you will dive deep into the inner workings of your mind and discover the hidden laws that govern your life. You will learn about the alchemy of the mind and how to harness its power to create positive change in your life and the world around you. Through the lens of Metaphysical philosophy, you will gain a new perspective on the world and your place in it. You will learn how the universe communicates with you through coded intelligence and how to unlock the hidden messages that are all around you.

This book is a journey for personal transformation and spiritual growth. Take a voyage of exploration of the expansive vistas of information discovering the codes of Metaphysics and the Quest of Life. You will learn the Metaphysical coded wisdom of the ancients for the necessary mind elements to transit into a higher mindset. Explore the secret relationship between the Earth and human beings, the higher mind, the Metaphysical journey, the importance of self, belief in self, the codes of mythology, a higher level of attainment, releasing the past, fears and evolving one's light on a Metaphysical level, what causes stress, work place promotion and why it does not happen, and many other topics. Included is a short overview of the conventional Twelve Laws of the Universe.

Book II. Decoding Thought
Welcome to a journey of self-discovery and exploration of the mysteries of the universe. "Decoding Thought" is a ground-breaking book that explores the power of the mind and the principles of metaphysical thought. Through a deep exploration of the mind and body connection, the author provides readers with insights to unlock the full potential of their thoughts. This book provides a guide to harnessing the power of the mind to create the life you desire. With explanations of metaphysical principles, the book makes these often complex concepts accessible to readers. "Decoding Thought" takes you on a journey through the vast landscape of the human mind. Explore the mysteries of thought power, and how it can shape our reality and transform our lives. The power of thought is not just a theoretical concept. It is a tangible force that can be harnessed to bring about significant changes in our lives.

This book can expand your consciousness and open your mind to new possibilities. By exploring the metaphysical principles that underlie our existence, you can gain a new perspective on life and the world around you. This book provides through a metaphysical interpretation explanations into the various aspects of thought power, including how it is linked to our DNA, and the roles played by the pituitary and pineal glands in our thought processes. O.M. Kelly also explains the metaphysical language in reference to the codes of the Egyptian Philosophies, the Bible, myths, cultures, and how they connect to the power of thought. The journey continues with a deep dive into the inner Secret School of Metaphysics, where we discover the Alchemy of the Brain and the pathway to our truth. Discover the unconscious/higher mind, and our Life Quest, which opens the doors to the Psychometric Consciousness. Through the lens of metaphysical interpretation, you will gain a new perspective on the impact of thought on our mental and emotional states that includes a look at Depression, Coping with Change and how to retrain our brain patterns to be positive and moving forward for our Financial Abundance and manifesting prosperity. The book ends with a brief overview of the brain/mind, and a short Q&A on thought power. This metaphysical book on the power of thought is a guide to discovering your true potential and creating the life you desire.

"Decoding Thought" is a must-read for anyone seeking to unlock the full potential of their mind and harness the power of the universe to create a life of fulfilment and this book serves as an invaluable resource.

Book III. Decoding Dis-Ease

Introducing "Decoding Dis-Ease" a Metaphysical Interpretation into understanding the intricate web of factors that contribute to our health and well-being. From the author of several groundbreaking works on the interaction of the mind and body, this book delves into a wide range of topics related to dis-ease. It is a fascinating and insightful book that offers a fresh perspective on health and healing. It is a must-read for anyone interested in the mind-body connection.

Readers will be inspired to embark on a quest of discovering the codes within themselves, recognizing that every cell in our body is pure Cosmic Consciousness. They will also gain a deeper understanding of specific health topics such as the thyroid, the kidneys, men's problems, and many other topics from a Metaphysical perspective. The book also examines how a dis-ease is given to us in group energy and the complex interplay between our bodies and minds, and how every human has the consequences of all that we do and experience.

Book IV. Decoding Death

Looking for a thought-provoking exploration of death and the afterlife? Look no further than O.M. Kelly's book, "Decoding Death".

"Decoding Death takes us on a transformative Metaphysical journey through the mysteries of the Universe. O.M. Kelly—known as Omni—provides an expanded horizon of possibilities, awareness, and a transformative perspective. In this book, Omni delves into a wide range of topics related to dying and death, from the loss of a loved one to a viewing of the afterlife. Omni has a unique ability to view the Laws of the Universe using her extraordinary state of heightened awareness and multi-dimensional perception and through the lens of metaphysics offers a unique perspective on the nature of death and what it means for the human experience.

Omni shares personal experiences and stories, including the passing of her late husband, brother, and parents, and offers a metaphysical insight for those dealing with loss and grief. She explores the transformational process of death and the potential for spiritual growth and enlightenment. The book explains that the human experience of death is part of a larger Universal process that is ultimately guided by a higher intelligence referred to as God (Laws of the Universe/Collective Consciousness) or whatever name you prefer. Omni's exploration of death is both metaphysically comprehensive and thought-provoking, offering readers a deep and nuanced understanding of one of life's greatest mysteries. With chapters on the Three Doorways—Three Stages of Death, The Quantum Hologram—Why a partner dies for the other partner to progress in the "Journey of Life", The Passing to the Afterlife, and many other enlightening chapters, "Decoding Death" offers a unique viewpoint. By drawing on a range of religious, philosophical, and metaphysical perspectives, Omni offers a compelling vision of the human experience of death and its role in the larger Universal Law.

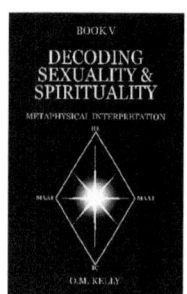

Book V. Decoding Sexuality And Spirituality

Welcome to "Decoding Sexuality and Spirituality" by O.M. Kelly. In this book, explore the fascinating relationship between our sexuality and spirituality, and how these two aspects of ourselves are intimately intertwined. Delve into the concept that sexuality is the doorway to our spirituality, and examine the powerful and transformative energy that is generated when we fully embrace our sexual selves. The book also explores the notion of the metaphysical orgasmic cloud, and how it can be used to deepen our connection to our spiritual selves. We will also examine the role of marriage in our sexual and spiritual lives.

For women, the book offers a unique perspective on the journey of embracing sexuality and spirituality, as well as insights into the different stages of life and how they impact our sexual and spiritual selves. Drawing on both ancient wisdom traditions and metaphysical mythology, the book examines the myth of Hercules and how it relates to our sexual intelligence. By decoding the symbolism of this myth, we can gain a deeper understanding of the ways in which our sexuality and spirituality intersect and influence each other. So if you are ready to embark on a journey of self-discovery and unlock the true potential of your sexual and spiritual selves, then "Decoding Sexuality and Spirituality" is the book for you.

VI. Decoding The Dolphin's Breath

"Decoding The Dolphin's Breath" by O.M. Kelly (Omni) is a captivating exploration of the relationship between humans and dolphins. The book begins with a poignant account of a real-life encounter between the author and a group of wild dolphins, setting the stage for a deep dive into the spiritual and metaphysical significance of dolphins. This captivating book takes readers on a journey into the heart of the dolphin-human relationship, exploring the ways in which these majestic creatures can help us attune to the power of free will, and telepathic communication.

Throughout the Laws of Shamanism the wonderful Dolphin in consciousness, represents the attainment we can reach through ourselves earning our freedom of will. This book explains the benefits of the dolphins breath—the why and how we use the breath that influences our divine mentality. Further, it's a story which reveals how the dolphins have taught us the process to be free of fear, and to tap into the Language of Babylon—to understand the language of Earth. One of the key themes of the book is the idea that dolphins are always breathing their total freedom of thought, and the author provides insights into how humans can learn from this remarkable trait. The book also invites readers to embark on a journey into understanding the telepathic communication of whales and dolphins. Inclusive in the book is a written meditation which assists you to connect to the external consciousness and release the fear that you have wrapped around yourself for protection.

Overall, this book offers a unique and fascinating perspective on the metaphysics of dolphins, and will appeal to anyone interested in spirituality, and the power of the mind.

Book VII. Decoding The Sacred Alphabet And Numerology

This book offers a myriad of explanations concerning the higher consciousness in relationship to names, places and numbers. "Decoding The Sacred Alphabet & Numerology" by O.M. Kelly (Omni) is a thought-provoking and enlightening read that

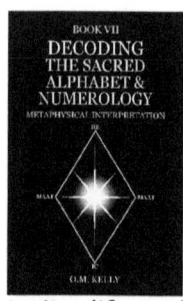

offers a unique perspective on the metaphysical world of letters and numbers.

Omni's insights and teachings are sure to inspire readers to deepen their understanding of the ancient sacred codes to names of places, your name and the sacred alphabet. The author also delves into the practice of metaphysical numerology, which involves using numerical values to interpret personality traits, life paths, and other aspects of a person's life. Omni explains how metaphysical numerology can be used to gain insight into our spiritual path and to better understand our purpose in life. Your ability to decipher the Sacred Alphabet and Numerology codes commonly and constantly presented to you throughout your life, will open opportunities to expand your consciousness and awareness you never thought possible.

Embark on a journey through the myth of Babylon and Shambhala and discover the sacred language that connects us all. Explore Luxor, the Delta Giza Saqqara and Faiyum, and Solomon's Temple, and uncover the mysteries of Akhenaton and Tomb KV-63. Find out how to unravel the threads of your DNA and unlock the ancient knowledge of the Old Aramaic Story of Aladdin and the Lamp. Explore Grecian stories through the Metaphysical language and travel along the Old Silk Road. Discover the Shamanic inheritance of numbers and their meanings, and learn how we rely on numbers to read the hidden language of the universe. Join O.M. Kelly on a journey of self-discovery and uncover the divine language within.

Book VIII. Decoding Sacred Fung Shwa

Introducing "Decoding Sacred Fung Shwa", the revolutionary guide to understanding and harnessing the energy within your home and yourself. In this book, author O.M. Kelly (Omni), has introduced a metaphysical sixth element that takes our understanding of energy to the next level. By incorporating "Your Life Force," we gain deeper insight into the connection between our homes and our emotional well-being. Discover the power of Fung Shwa and learn how to use it to create a balanced and harmonized environment that supports your mind, body, and Soul.

The book explains the meaning of Sacred Fung Shwa to the Shamanistic principles that underpin it. Delve into the metaphysical medicine wheel and explore the elements of life, before moving on to practical applications of Fung Shwa in the home.

Learn how to visualize your home as a collective energy and clear the clutter to enhance its flow. Discover your Astrological colours and how they can be used in Fung Shwa design, from the kitchen to the bedroom and beyond. Explore the compatibility of personal colours in relationships, and discover the power of paintings, pictures, and mirrors to enhance your home's energy.

But Fung Shwa isn't just about the home—we also explore its applications in the office environment and in small retail businesses. Learn how to apply Fung Shwa principles to a clothing store, shoe store, or café, even discover the role of Fung Shwa in money, and to Metaphysical Numerology.

Throughout it all, we focus on the quest of life and how Fung Shwa can help you achieve your goals and live your best life. So what are you waiting for? Dive into the world of Fung Shwa and transform your home, your business, and your life today!

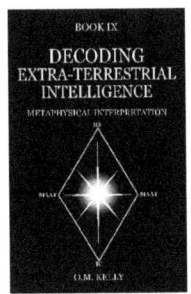

Book IX. Decoding Extra-Terrestrial Intelligence
Are you ready to embark on a journey of self-discovery? Look no further than O.M. Kelly's groundbreaking book, Book IX "Decoding Extra-Terrestrial Intelligence". Through metaphysical interpretation, O.M. Kelly (Omni) has unlocked the secrets of the universe and revealed that the key to our next step in human evolution lies within ourselves. This book will show you how to tap into the indelible imprint of holographic importance that is seeded within every human, and unleash the Extra-Terrestrial Intelligence that resides within you. Omni shares her own personal journey of encountering Beings of Light and how it has transformed her understanding of the universe and humanity's place within it.

Omni presents the concept that we all have Extra-Terrestrial Intelligence, and have the ability to tap into the vast knowledge and secrets of the universe. The ancient civilizations left behind clues and teachings about this metaphysical existence and it is up to us to continue to uncover and advance the way we think. Through this journey of life, we can unlock the secrets of our own consciousness and tap into the full potential of our existence. This is a fascinating exploration of the mysteries of the universe and the potential for our own personal evolution.

Readers who are interested in self-transformation through universal truths, Metaphysical exploration for personal growth and a journey of self-discovery would be interested in reading this insightful book on contact with Beings of Light and Extra-terrestrial Intelligence, exploring ancient civilizations and the knowledge they possessed about the universe and the human mind.

Power Thought for the Day Oracle Book

"Power Thought For The Day Oracle Book" provides insights to assist you on your life path. Through the "Totem" energy of all, the ancient species that have evolved before us, represent an emotional inheritance that we can rely on to sustain the moment. Each species that has evolved on this planet is recorded into our cellular memory. This book with 22 Major Arcana Shamanic Power Animal Totems provides a contemporary metaphysical interpretation symbolic of our evolution. By selecting a page of the book the Shamanic animal will provide an insight in how you are thinking at this moment in time. Through the contemporary Laws of Shamanism (with a metaphysical interpretation), O.M. Kelly (Omni) has produced a book that will assist the "Path of the Initiate" in emotional intelligence when our mind is in the field of doubt. When we become aware of how we are thinking it is a catalyst for transformation. This compact little book is a handy 4 x 7 inches or 10.2 x 17.8 cm to fit into your pocket or handbag.

How to use the book:
Our higher mind has no time; it steps into and works on behalf of the thought of the moment. This book encompasses 22 Major Totem Power representations, symbolic of our evolution. Close your eyes and inhale and exhale a deep breath and relax and allow yourself no thought as you select the right page of the Shamanic animal presented in this book. The right page will always appear for you at the right moment and you will discover how the power animals are working with you for insight into their wisdom. Different power animals come into our lives at various phases offering messages to guide us on our path.

Decoding the Shaman Within

In "Decoding the Shaman Within" international author O.M. Kelly (Omni) shares her Shamanic metaphysical journey. It would be termed a contemporary Shamanic initiation journey; a powerful spiritual enlightenment and transformational voyage of discovering the codes of Metaphysics and the Quest of Life. Through the sacred passage of time Omni discovered the secret codes of the Collective Consciousness (Laws of the Universe) to trek a higher level of consciousness.

Throughout Omni's training to receive the breath of Shamanism, many Elders from other cultures came to Australia and initiated her into their own tribal laws. Most of these Elders were men who arrived on Omni's doorstep uninvited but had received the call from the Universe to pass on their knowledge. Those magnificent people who had also earned their Shamanic experiences, only stayed long enough to give Omni their gift of consciousness and to initiate her into a new Shamanic name, which their tribe had bestowed, and then they disappeared out of Omni's life as quickly as they had come into it.

The Shamanic path in a Metaphysical perspective is the oldest pathway of the tribal law through the evolution of humanity. The Shaman is trained in the ancient language that is instilled in every genetic code that humanity carries within their DNA; you either have the opportunity to open it up and use it, or you just don't bother and choose to ignore it! It is as simple as that!

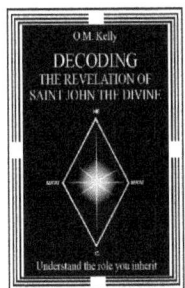

Decoding the Revelation of Saint John the Divine: Understand the role you inherit

The amazing breakthrough book "Decoding the Revelation of Saint John the Divine: Understand the role you inherit", is for anyone with an open, inquiring mind, seeking answers to the surreal descriptions of Earth's final days.

Through years of research O.M. Kelly interprets the cryptology behind the codes of mythology and various religions and has Metaphysically interpreted how the Holy Bible had been written through the original codex of Egyptology. The biblical stories were collected and condensed through the educated minds of that time.

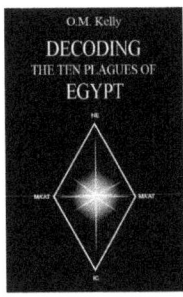

Decoding the Ten Plagues of Egypt

"Decoding the Ten Plagues of Egypt" presents a fresh insight into understanding the hidden structure of the language of how the Bible was written. The reader is introduced to the step by step Metaphysical decoding of the mystifying language, regarding the plagues from the Book of Exodus, Chapters: 7-12 in the Bible.

For the first time in contemporary history the essence of the Book of Exodus and its previously unsolved intriguing language will be revealed to provide deeper knowledge and clearer perception to unlock the significance the Book of Exodus is explaining to us.

Decoding Dreams

In "Decoding Dreams" international author O.M. Kelly (Omni), introduces a metaphysical interpretation of the dreams we dream. At times, we may believe that dreams allow us to peer into another world. O.M. Kelly provides the codes for us to understand that other world of dreams—or, through the Shamanic Principles, our "Vision Worlds". Dreams are created through your unconscious/higher mind communicating back to you; dreams are reminding you of the lessons that you need to understand regarding yourself. You cannot hear them if your mind is filled with incessant chatter. The ego refuses to conform when it is in control of the moment. Dreams can range from a pleasant dream, which could be a recommendation to add to what you are doing, to a nightmare, which is a wake-up call from your higher self regarding what you are doing to yourself. As you read this book, keep in mind that learning to metaphysically interpret your dreams is a step-by-step process. Areas covered in the book are: Dream Representations (Animal Kingdom and the Human Kingdom), Questions and Answers about Dreams, and Dream Interpretations.

Reprint coming in the near future.

NOTES:

www.ingramcontent.com/pod-product-compliance
Lightning Source LLC
Chambersburg PA
CBHW051539010526
44107CB00064B/2788